The PRISMAS Group Therapy Handbook

Bruno Luiz Avelino Cardoso
Ana Clara Gomes Braga

The PRISMAS Group Therapy Handbook

A Brief Intervention Integrating Affirmative and Schema Therapy for Sexual and Gender Minorities

Springer

Bruno Luiz Avelino Cardoso
Laboratory for Studies and Interventions in Cognitive and Contextual Therapies
Federal University of Minas Gerais
Belo Horizonte, Minas Gerais, Brazil

Ana Clara Gomes Braga
Laboratory for Studies and Interventions in Cognitive and Contextual Therapies
Federal University of Minas Gerais
Belo Horizonte, Minas Gerais, Brazil

ISBN 978-3-031-91808-7 ISBN 978-3-031-91809-4 (eBook)
https://doi.org/10.1007/978-3-031-91809-4

The original submitted manuscript has been translated into English. The translation was done using artificial intelligence. A subsequent revision was performed by the author(s) to further refine the work and to ensure that the translation is appropriate concerning content and scientific correctness. It may, however, read stylistically different from a conventional translation.

This Springer imprint is published by the registered company Springer Nature Switzerland AG
The registered company address is: Gewerbestrasse 11, 6330 Cham, Switzerland

Foreword I

Having worked in Schema Therapy, and alongside Jeffrey Young, for decades, I have witnessed a profound capacity to help individuals connect with their deepest needs. The theoretical and practical foundations of Schema Therapy not only stand strong on their own but also integrate seamlessly with other psychological approaches. As research continues, we are further solidifying its status as an evidence-based model applicable to various issues.

When Bruno invited me to write the Foreword for his new book, I immediately recognized it as a significant and timely contribution to Schema Therapy. While the model offers a broad range of applications, there remains a gap in understanding how its principles apply to minority groups, including LGBTQIA+ individuals. Bruno's work in this area is groundbreaking. His research on minority stress and the inner critic (oppressive sociocultural) schema mode sheds light on how societal influences shape individual experiences, schemas, and modes. His dedication to this topic within Schema Therapy has yielded invaluable insights into the sociocultural dimensions of working with minority populations. Bruno is a masterful schema therapist and a thoughtfully articulate writer—this book will prove to be an essential resource.

It is with great enthusiasm that I introduce ***The PRISMAS Group Therapy Handbook: A Brief Intervention Integrating Affirmative and Schema Therapy for Sexual and Gender Minorities***. This pioneering work by Bruno and Ana represents a crucial advancement in both Affirmative and Schema Therapy, providing essential support for sexual and gender minorities.

In today's world, where diversity and inclusion are more important than ever, the need for effective, tailored therapeutic interventions cannot be overstated. The PRISMAS manual stands out as the first of its kind—not just offering theoretical insights but also presenting a structured, practical framework that merges the principles of Schema Therapy with well-established affirmative practices.

The book takes readers on a structured journey through the therapeutic process, from initial sessions that build self-awareness and connection to intermediate strategies that empower clients to challenge internalized critic modes and embrace their true identities. This progression culminates in consolidation and celebration, ensuring that therapy not only addresses struggles but also fosters resilience, self-acceptance, and personal growth.

This powerful intervention is a vital resource for professionals worldwide working with LGBTQIAP+ populations. By addressing minority stress and internalized prejudice, the handbook provides validation, healing, and a pathway to empowerment. Bruno and Ana's work demonstrates the transformative potential of integrating Schema Therapy with Affirmative Therapy, turning negative patterns into opportunities for connection, strength, and self-acceptance.

As mental health professionals, we have a responsibility to expand our knowledge and clinical practice to include the diverse experiences of all individuals. This manual is a significant step in that direction, equipping clinicians with invaluable tools to create affirming and effective therapeutic spaces. I wholeheartedly support this endeavor and look forward to seeing the positive impact it will have on both clients and practitioners.

The International Society of Schema Therapy (ISST) Wendy Behary
Bad Vilbel, Germany

The Cognitive Therapy Center of NJ
Springfield, NJ, USA

The Schema Therapy Institutes of NJ-NYC-DC
Springfield, NJ, USA

Author of Disarming the Narcissist and Deliberate Practice in Schema Therapy

Foreword II

> Queerness is a gift, a soft rupture against the world's rigid order. It is not rebellion nor spectacle, but the slow work of finding room to breathe. In this struggle, something emerges—not freedom, but the possibility of it.

In early 2023, while organizing a symposium on adaptations of Schema Therapy to address the psychological effects of discrimination and social exclusion, I found myself grappling with a pressing question: why does psychotherapy so often overlook how deeply society shapes mental health?

This question brought to light a recurring issue within the field. Many, like myself, who have trained in Clinical Psychology or similar fields are taught the bio-psycho-social model—a framework that acknowledges the biological, psychological, and social determinants of well-being. Yet, in practice, the "bio" is often handed off to psychiatrists, the "social" to sociologists and anthropologists, while therapists focus narrowly on the psychological. This compartmentalization misses something essential: the interconnectedness of these dimensions and the enduring imprint of sociocultural forces on mental health.

I deeply felt that Schema Therapy provides the potential to bridge these dimensions as a complex and integrative model. By addressing how social exclusion, discrimination, and bias profoundly shape early experiences—and how schemas and modes are maintained by their ongoing impact—we can connect the dots between the personal and the societal.

It was in this state of inquiry that I encountered Bruno Cardoso and his colleagues' groundbreaking work with individuals who identify as sexual and gender minorities (SGM—a term used within the medical and scientific community referring to LGBTQIA+ people). All the way from Brazil, their insights arrived as if summoned by my questions, bringing clarity to the swirling ideas in my mind. Their conceptualization of the Inner Critic (Oppressive Sociocultural) Schema Mode crystallized what I had long felt: that societal oppression leaves a distinct and enduring mark on the mental health of marginalized communities around the world. It also underscored the critical need for psychotherapy to actively address internalized oppression. Furthermore, healing or integration of the Healthy Adult mode includes fostering community connection and pride in one's identity.

Reflecting on LGBTQIA+ history, I am reminded of how collective struggles for recognition have shaped not just individual lives but the field of mental health itself. Until just 50 years ago, homosexuality was classified as a mental illness, embedding societal biases into the very systems meant to promote well-being. The removal of homosexuality from the *Diagnostic and Statistical Manual of Mental Disorders* (DSM) in 1973 marked a pivotal shift away from pathologization and toward societal acceptance. Yet, progress for transgender and gender-diverse individuals has been far slower. The DSM-V reclassified Gender Dysphoria in 2013, framing it as distress caused by incongruence rather than an inherent disorder. While the World Health Organization further depathologized gender incongruence in the ICD-11 in 2019, systemic barriers and increasing anti-trans legislation remind us how far we are from achieving true equity. These historical shifts still shape how mental health systems engage with LGBTQIA+ clients today.

These systemic challenges raise profound questions: How do you thrive when society tells you that you are defective or deranged—or that you don't exist at all? How do you develop a sense of worthiness when the world imposes crushing limits on who you can be—whether as a child, a professional, a parent, or simply a loved and loving person? These questions are not just theoretical; they remain at the heart of so many clients' lived experiences.

Thankfully, the shift toward Sexual and Gender Affirmative models of care has moved away from the outdated notion of "fixing" LGBTQIA+ people. Instead, these models prioritize self-determination, validation, empowerment, cultural humility, and trauma-informed practice. By addressing the systemic and relational impacts of oppression, they emphasize understanding the unique experiences of LGBTQIA+ clients and the broader forces contributing to their distress. In this way, affirming and effective care naturally aligns with the principles of Schema Therapy. At its heart, it focuses on attuning to clients' realities and validating their lived experiences.

This is what makes *The PRISMAS Group Therapy Handbook* so vital in addressing these deeply important and complex questions for SGM clients. Bruno and Ana present a framework that is both sexual and gender affirming. It resonates across borders by addressing the shared experiences of minority stress, internalized oppression, and systemic barriers faced by SGM communities worldwide. By bridging societal oppression with individual healing, their approach fully leverages the integrative potential of Schema Therapy.

I encourage you to read this book not just as a guide to effective therapy but as an invitation to fully embrace the richness of LGBTQIA+ lives. These communities are a vibrant tapestry of resilience, creativity, and complexity, shaped by intersections of identity and experience.

Bruno and Ana's work is a gift to the field of psychotherapy, and it is a privilege to introduce it to you. May it inspire you to create spaces where LGBTQIA+ communities can not only survive but also thrive.

SchemXcollective: Integrative Schema Institute Xi Liu
Sydney, NSW, Australia

Preface

This manual is intended to provide guidance for therapists responsible for conducting the PRISMAS Program. With the intention of ensuring an appropriate and careful application of this therapeutic group, each session will be detailed, presenting objectives and procedures, with some activities featuring narrated examples and/or images for didactic purposes. Detailed tables will be provided with the estimated duration of each session, to ensure that the thought structure is applied in practice.

The fundamental purpose of this manual is to empower therapists, developing a deep understanding of the needs and challenges faced by sexual and gender minorities (SGM), thus contributing to an inclusive and affirmative therapeutic environment. For this, various concepts of Schema Therapy (ST) and about sexual diversity will be explored during the sessions, to achieve a good understanding of the theory that underpins the activities. The focus is on that even a therapist who is not so familiar with these themes could be able to obtain the necessary knowledge for the application of the program through the reading of the manual. They will be able to use the knowledge acquired here in their practice, performing more inclusive and careful services with the SGM population.

Working with SGM can be challenging for several reasons. One of them is that the stress internalized by these people is very high, since they live in a stigmatizing culture, where they receive various microaggressions from social structures—such as the difficulty, for example, of finding a doctor who does not repeat prejudiced or invalidating speeches (Meyer, 2003). Often, this population does not have adequate care networks, dealing with situations of social distancing and the feeling of isolation and defectiveness. Therefore, bringing together members of the LGBTQIA+ community in a group boosts the start of forming healthier bonds, in the face of a culture of stigma. It allows to combat internalized homo/bi/transphobia and generate a higher quality of life. This alone is already a tool for change. But it is possible to go further, with knowledge more grounded in modern psychological science.

The main theoretical basis of the PRISMAS intervention is Schema Therapy (ST). That is, a contemporary modality of psychotherapy that has been accumulating evidence over the years. It is indicated for a deepening in the interventions of classical Cognitive-Behavioral Therapy, also bringing the patient's past and previous experiences to the center of the intervention (Young et al., 2003). There are protocols being tested to expand this approach beyond individual clinical practice, with Group ST interventions (GST) already being consolidated to intervene in various complaints, such as people with Borderline Personality Disorder (Farrell & Shaw, 2012).

Combining the two areas of knowledge (from the field of sexual diversity and ST), the program seeks to provide possibilities for group intervention also for transdiagnostic aspects, that is, those that are present in some populations regardless of a specific diagnosis—this is the case of minority stress and internalized homo/bi/transphobia in SGM. This is because one of the proposals of ST is to expand cognitive-behavioral therapy to encompass patients who could not be fully contemplated by the linear and diagnosis-focused models of CBT, being multi-complaint or resistant to change. This is a way to remove SGM from the place of pathologization, without denying, however, their varied and unique needs for care in the face of psychological suffering to which they are exposed in a homophobic and transphobic world. In addition, the manual offers guidelines for maintaining and improving well-being and quality of life, moving away from the logic of symptom treatment that many protocols for this population follow.

Thinking, still, about the need to expand the support network of these people and ensure that they feel validated and understood by peers with similar experiences, meeting other SGM in a safe environment and mediated by trained professionals can be a potent therapeutic support. Unlike other minorities, such as women and black people, they do not have constant and direct contact with peers, as many people in the LGBTQIA+ group hide their own sexuality to avoid aggression and attacks. Thus, working on this feeling of loneliness and inadequacy is even more facilitated when bringing together people with similar stories. Limited reparenting, an important validation strategy in ST, has plenty of room in this context, opening various possibilities for care and emotional support.

It is also worth noting that this program also combines contextual aspects with ST, proposing experiences of emotional regulation that address not only the content of cognitions, but also the way these thoughts occur, analyzing the phenomenon in a broader way. Also, it integrates knowledge from Affirmative Therapy, considering the already present consolidation of groups with affirmative practices for SGM, with relevant and promising results (Craig et al., 2021). Despite integrating different interventions thinking about what is most relevant in science, at the present moment, for the care with SGM, the theoretical and epistemological bases follow the model of Young's ST (Young et al., 2003), highlighting from this the Inner Critic (Oppressive Sociocultural) Mode and the Affirmative Healthy Adult (Cardoso et al., 2022) as two entities that summarize, in many ways, the dysfunctional and functional experiences, respectively, of this population. Disempowering/Combating this first, reducing schematic activations, thought traps, and self-criticism is one of the main objectives. Also, strengthening the second, to generate well-being, emotional regulation, and functional coping strategies is an essential complement. Finally, for the pursuit of greater overall well-being, child modes and coping modes are also addressed.

In summary, this manual follows the precepts of ST to generate cognitive, behavioral, and emotional changes. It addresses aspects relevant to the experience of minorities and is culturally sensitive. It is hoped that going through this intervention will be a resource to increase self-knowledge and generate a reduction in stress, anxiety, and depression, promoting more well-being in the life of a group that so much needs it, but historically has little access to resources.

References

Cardoso, B. L. A., Paim, K., Catelan, R. F., & Liebross, E. H. (2022). Minority stress and the inner critic/oppressive sociocultural schema mode among sexual and gender minorities. *Current Psychology, 42*, 19991–19999. https://doi.org/10.1007/s12144-022-03086-y

Craig, S. L., Leung, V. W. Y., Pascoe, R., Pang, N., Iacono, G., Austin, A., & Dillon, F. (2021). AFFIRM Online: utilizing an affirmative cognitive-behavioral digital intervention to improve mental health, access, and engagement among LGBTQA+ youth and young adults. *International Journal of Environment Research and Public Health, 18*(4).

Farrell, J. M., & Shaw, I. A. (2012). *Group schema therapy for borderline personality disorder: A step-by-step treatment manual with patient workbook*. Wiley-Blackwell.

Meyer, I. H. (2003). Prejudice, social stress, and mental health in lesbian, gay, and bisexual populations: Conceptual issues and research evidence. *Psychological Bulletin, 129*(5), 674–697. https://doi.org/10.1037/0033-2909.129.5.674

Young, J. E., Klosko, J. S., & Weishaar, M. E. (2003). *Schema therapy: A practitioner's guide*. Guilford Press.

Belo Horizonte, Minas Gerais, Brazil

Bruno Luiz Avelino Cardoso
Ana Clara Gomes Braga

Competing Interests The authors have no competing interests to declare that are relevant to the content of this manuscript.

Contents

1 Introduction 1

Part I Initial Sessions: Understanding Schema Therapy and My Internal Way of Functioning

2 "Connecting with My Network and Understanding My Way of Functioning": Bond Creation and Self-monitoring 15

3 "Getting to Know my Different Sides": Presentation of Modes 25

4 "How Society Influenced the Criticisms That I Internalized About Myself": Inner Critic Modes, Minority Stress, and Prejudice Against Sexual and Gender Diversity 37

5 "Knowing and Highlighting My Strengths": Strengthening the Affirmative Healthy Adult Mode 49

6 "Connecting with My History": Deepening Self-knowledge About How What I Went Through Influenced Who I Am 57

Part II Intermediate Sessions: Changing My Way of Thinking, Acting, and Feeling Through the Integration of Schema Therapy and Affirmative Therapy

7 "I Think, Therefore I (Do Not) Criticize Myself": Cognitive Strategies for Coping with the Inner Critic (Oppressive Sociocultural) Mode 65

8 "The Child Who Lives in Me": Welcoming the Child Modes 75

9 "Where Does This Internal Storm Come From? Understanding My Emotions": Emotion-Focused Strategies for Understanding and Regulating Various Modes 83

10 "Allowing Myself a New Way of Feeling": Experiential Strategies for Coping with the Inner Critic (Oppressive Sociocultural) Mode 91

11 "Acting as the Person I Aspire to Be": Behavioral Strategies for Coping with the Inner Critic (Oppressive Sociocultural) Mode 99

Part III Final Sessions: Consolidating and Strengthening My Affirmative Healthy Adult and Having Fun with My Happy Child

12 "Connecting Our Individual Strengths to Health and Affirmation": Building the Healthy Adult Connected to the Social Group 111

13 "Releasing the Happy Child": Allowing the Expression of Creativity and Fun for the Group's Closure 119

14 Final Considerations 125

Appendix I: Brief Description of Schema Modes 129

Appendix II: Mind Map of the Inner Critic (Oppressive Sociocultural) Mode 131

Appendix III: Coping Card 133

Appendix IV: Characteristics of the Healthy Adult 135

Appendix V: Brief Summary of the Five Core Emotional Needs (CENs) 137

Appendix VI: Thought Traps 139

Appendix VII: Color Emotion Diary 143

Appendix VIII: Thought Record 145

Appendix XIX: Brief Summary of the 18 Early Maladaptive Schemas 147

Index 149

Chapter 1
Introduction

It is likely that a therapist who decides to read this manual is interested in the themes of Schema Therapy (ST) and sexual and gender diversity. This is a very positive sign, and the fact that these areas are being seen and studied reflects a significant social change. However, as they are still relatively new spaces within psychology, it is natural that knowledge about these themes varies quite a bit. Perhaps some professionals fully understand the functioning of ST, but have never worked directly with sexual and gender minorities (SGM). Similarly, people who have dedicated their lives to the study and intervention with SGM may have little or no contact with ST or with Cognitive-Behavioral Therapies in general. Considering that some of the values of this intervention are accessibility, collaboration, and a genuine and affirmative stance, the manual was created to be welcoming and didactic also for the therapists themselves.

Although reading does not replace advanced training or a more in-depth reading in these areas, the manual provides the initial bases to understand how to integrate ST and Affirmative Therapy with SGM. The objectives and procedures of each activity are explained and application tips are offered. The purpose is that interested professionals can learn valid techniques and perform an easy-to-follow intervention in a brief group therapy session for this population. Even if they do not apply the group intervention itself, they can adopt these resources in their individual practices, understanding how to contextualize the techniques described in their own clinical practice. In addition, they can better understand specific needs of SGM and offer more appropriate services, reducing the chances of committing microaggressions.

Before the step-by-step description of how to apply the program, however, some key concepts are important. This introduction aims to present these concepts in a simple and direct way. It can be revisited at any time, in case doubts arise during reading. The chapters of each session also include detailed guide texts on the topics covered, to facilitate understanding of the content. In this section of the book, ST will be described: what are schemas and how early maladaptive schemas (EMSs)

B. L. A. Cardoso, A. C. G. Braga, *The PRISMAS Group Therapy Handbook*,
https://doi.org/10.1007/978-3-031-91809-4_1

are formed. In the SGM issue, the topic covered is: what are modes and what is the theory behind the internalized critical (sociocultural oppressor) mode.

What Are Schemas?

The concept of schemas has been studied in various fields of psychology. From developmental psychology, by Piaget (1952), to cognitive therapies, including Beck's work (1976), understanding schemas has served both as motivation for research and as a basis for structuring interventions. ST is one of the psychological models dedicated to this concept, structuring both its theoretical and practical basis (Young et al., 2003).

Generally, schemas can be described as a set of sensations, thoughts, and emotions that the human brain uses to understand an idea or concept. For example, a small child who always interacts with a pet from birth begins to try to understand it. They hear adults call that animal a dog. Soon, they gather the information: "if it barks, has four legs, tickles me when it licks me and turns its belly for me to pet, it's a dog." This categorization facilitates access to and understanding of the world around them, that is, the child spends less energy formulating hypotheses and logical propositions, as they managed to group distinct parts into a congruent whole. With maturity, this child begins to perceive inconsistencies in their generalizations and creates more refined and useful schemas. "If it meows and is smaller and with sharper ears, it's not a dog, but a cat" (Papalia & Feldman, 2011).

Life experiences can reinforce or not the formed schema. Perhaps this child meets the neighbor's dog that is quiet and does not like to lick or turn its belly. This would make them review the idea of what this animal is. However, if most dogs are lively and open, she will probably keep their concept, being more certain that it is closer to a useful truth.

It's easy to think about schemas when the subject is objects or concrete beings. Most humans will have a similar view of what a dog or cat is. However, schemas are also formed for abstract ideas: "what is love, a friendship, the meaning of life?" In this case, the formulations can vary according to life history, culture, and family experience. A person who grew up in a warm home, where they were loved and cherished just for existing, may understand love as "the affection we naturally have for those around us." Someone who lived in an environment where they had to strive a lot to receive affection, being frequently criticized, may have a more distorted view of the same theme: "love is what we receive if we don't make mistakes and strive a lot." Thus, these schemas can be either maladaptive (early maladaptive schemas), when they bring harm and maintain self-defeating patterns, or adaptive (early adaptive schemas), when they bring positive and healthier outcomes for the individual (Young et al., 2003).

It should be noted that schemas are also influenced by personality, a person's way of being. This way of being is formed by the interaction between basic tendencies and the experiences that a person undergoes over time, resulting in a mix between the innate and the learned. The most accepted model by the scientific community, currently, to explain personality is the "Big Five Model," or Big Five. It describes five-dimensional domains that all people have in to some degree. These traits are inherited at birth and remain relatively stable throughout life. And so while it is unlikely that a psychotherapeutic intervention will alter these basic tendencies, psychology can teach important skills to maximize the potential of who one is and compensate for challenges. The five traits can be summarized according to Costa and McCrae (1992):

1. Openness to experiences: Refers to a person's interest in experiencing new things or considering different ideas. People with low openness tend to be more conservative, preferring routine and continuity, while those with high openness appreciate changes and diversity of ideas and experiences.
2. Conscientiousness: Refers to the tendency to act in a planned, organized, and methodical way. People with high conscientiousness tend to be more responsible and dedicated, although they may also exhibit psychological rigidity. Those with low levels of this trait tend to procrastinate or become disorganized about their tasks.
3. Extraversion: In addition to social connection, this trait also relates to someone's energy level. Highly extroverted people enjoy company and have a lot of energy and vitality. On the other hand, more introverted individuals, in addition to preferring the company of a few good friends, tend to tire more easily from social activities.
4. Agreeableness: Refers to a person's pro-social tendency. This trait speaks about empathy and concern for others, not necessarily about desiring closeness. Highly agreeable people usually pay a lot of attention to others and take care of them, although they may appear naive in certain situations. Those with lower levels of this trait tend to be more self-centered and suspicious of the intentions of others.
5. Neuroticism: Relates to the way someone deals with challenging emotions. People with high neuroticism tend to suffer more from stress and frustration, while those with low neuroticism tend to be more stable and calm, although they may not be as attentive to risks and dangers.

It should be noted that there is no good or bad personality. All traits can be useful or not, depending on the context. For example, high neuroticism, although it can cause suffering in modern societies, was crucial for survival in the Stone Age, as it allowed attention to risks and a greater chance of escaping from predators. The traits need to be analyzed according to the context and their interaction with someone's schemas. Possibly, a person with low openness will need more stimulation to express themselves and engage in new experiences than someone who naturally seeks them out. They may have a greater tendency to internalize early maladaptive schemas such as emotional inhibition (not clearly expressing what they need and little contact with their own feelings) or unrelenting standards (rigid ways of performing tasks), if they do not have caregivers attentive to their individual needs. Although all people need to have their core emotional needs met, the intensity of attention that each one requires varies according to their personality.

How Are Early Maladaptive Schemas Formed?

Just as there are different people with varied stories and personalities, the schemas that these people form also vary. Some schemas can be healthy or neutral, as already mentioned. Understanding "what is a dog" or "how should I behave at a party" is necessary for the brain to assimilate information quickly and practically. However, some schemas can make people's lives difficult and cause intense suffering. In ST, they are called Early Maladaptive Schemas. They form when a person's core emotional needs are not adequately met during the early stages of life, such as in childhood and adolescence. Usually, caregivers are responsible for meeting these needs, although other areas, such as school, culture, and peers, are also relevant. Below is a summary of each of the five core emotional needs (Rafaeli et al., 2011; Young et al., 2003):

1. Secure attachment/connection: The fundamental need for security, to be accepted and cared for, essential for mental health and human development. Lack of secure attachment in childhood can result in emotional difficulties and relationship problems in adult life.
2. Autonomy/competence and sense of identity: The child needs to explore the world and develop their abilities, with the support of caregivers to foster their independence. Overprotection can generate insecure adults and with difficulties in problem-solving and decision-making.
3. Realistic limits and self-control: The need to understand and follow social rules for healthy coexistence. Excesses or lack of limits can lead to rigidity or permissiveness, affecting the ability to handle responsibilities in adult life.
4. Emotional validation and freedom to express: The importance of emotional regulation and the expression of emotions without fear of repression. The appropriate support during childhood and adolescence promotes self-confidence and the ability to deal with difficult feelings in adult life.
5. Spontaneity and play: Essential for the development of an authentic identity, allowing the exploration of hobbies and social interactions. Lack of spontaneity and play can lead to a pessimistic and worried view of life in adulthood.

EMSs are the focus of clinicians and researchers in ST for quite some time. Although there are several categorizations to define them (Arntz et al., 2021; Bach et al., 2017; Young et al., 2003), there is currently consensus to consider 18 EMSs, which are common to human experience. They are described in Table 1.1.

Table 1.1 Early maladaptive schemas and their definitions

Early Maladaptive Schemas: Rigid and maladaptive interpretive cognitive structures, used broadly and always linked to strong emotional activation. There are 18 schemas, distributed into five groups (Domains) according to their origin	
1. Emotional deprivation	Feelings and beliefs of loneliness, helplessness, and lack of understanding
2. Abandonment/Instability	Belief that you will lose the loved one and will not be able to stand being alone
3. Mistrust/Abuse	Expectation that others will intentionally harm you
4. Defectiveness/Shame	Belief of being defective, worthless, and unworthy of being loved
5. Social isolation/Alienation	Feeling of not belonging and being different from others
6. Failure	Beliefs that your performance is inferior to that of your peers
7. Dependence/incompetence	Beliefs of being unable to solve problems on your own
8. Vulnerability to harm or illness	Beliefs of being vulnerable to diseases and possible catastrophes
9. Enmeshment/Underdeveloped self	Feeling of not being able to individualize from parents and others
10. Entitlement/Grandiosity	Beliefs of being superior to other people and deserving privileges
11. Insufficient self-control/Self-discipline	Emphasis on relief of discomfort, at the expense of achievements and care
12. Self-sacrifice	Belief that you must always satisfy others
13. Subjugation	Concern about pleasing to avoid being rejected or retaliated against
14. Approval-seeking/Recognition-seeking	Belief that you will only have value if you have the approval of others
15. Emotional inhibition	Intense inhibition of feelings, actions, and communication
16. Unrelenting standards	Belief that you must always do and be the best
17. Negativity/Pessimism	Extreme focus on the negative aspects of life
18. Punitiveness	Belief that people need to be punished for their mistakes

Source: Paim et al. (2020, p. 79)

What Are Schema Modes and What Is the Theory Behind the Inner Critic (Oppressive Sociocultural) Mode?

The schema modes refer to a highly relevant concept in ST. The schemas are multiple and varied, which can make it difficult to understand both for patients and for therapists when presenting them in psychotherapy. Thus, modes would be ways of functioning that are classically observed in a clinical setting. Each person would have, within themselves, parts that manifest in certain situations—a healthier side that emerges when needed to work or take care of something: a more vulnerable side that seeks connection, among others. Modes are formed by sets of schemas and ways of dealing with them. Therefore, they are made up of memories, thoughts, sensations, emotions, and behaviors activated simultaneously (Rafaeli et al., 2011; Young et al., 2003). Each mode and its impact on mental health are best described in the PRISMAS sessions, including the coping strategies that are used in the face of schemas.

For this intervention, the main focus is the inner critic (oppressive sociocultural) mode. It was presented by Cardoso et al. (2022), when this group of researchers sought to theorize how the experiences of SGM in a culture of prejudice toward diversity could impact the suffering and mental health of this audience. The inner critic modes, as a whole, already make up a concept used since the foundations of ST. They represent the critical and punitive messages internalized by a person during their development, forming a relentless internal critic (Young et al., 2003). This mode is present in all those who have been exposed to excessive criticism (whether by caregivers, schoolmates, or specific figures).

The inner critic (oppressive sociocultural) mode, then, would be a broad version of the inner critic mode, specific to SGM (and/or marginalized social groups), mainly due to the internalization of sociocultural aspects that are the basis of prejudice against sexual and gender diversity, or prejudice against marginalized social groups (Cardoso & Campos, 2023). This mode is impacted by aspects of micro and macro culture, and is influenced by distal stressors (i.e., external to the person), such as experiences of discrimination or prejudice, experiences of victimization and violence, living in a country with laws that restrict rights, and family or social rejection for being an LGBTQIA+ person (Cardoso et al., 2022).

For Cardoso et al. (2022), the inner critic (oppressive sociocultural) mode is formed by the EMSs, coping strategies, and emotional states in the face of these experiences, along with the proximal stressors (internalized aspects of the oppressive society). This internalization includes prejudice against sexual and gender diversity, concealment of identity, negative expectations and, in the case of trans people, gender dysphoria, rumination about one's own body, and concerns about "passing" (how much the person is visually perceived as being of the gender they define). Having such a mode activated in an intense way generates outcomes such as physical and mental health problems and lower well-being. However, some resilience factors may be the key to a healthier progression: connection to the community and pride. These factors are best evidenced in Fig. 1.1.

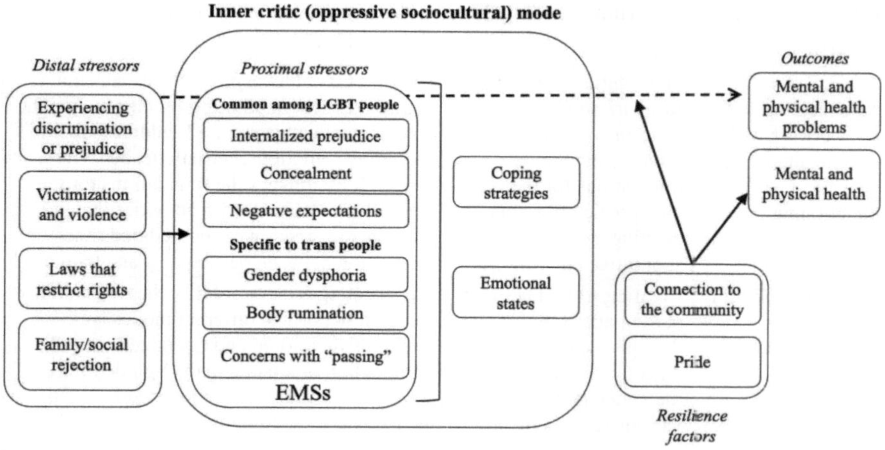

Fig. 1.1 Understanding of the inner critic (oppressive sociocultural) mode. *Source*: Cardoso et al. (2022)

In summary, this mode involves the internalization of diffuse messages of oppression and prejudice against sexual and gender diversity, generating self-deprecating beliefs and negative judgments about oneself. This mode can lead to excessive self-demand, perfectionism, and low self-esteem, with a particular focus on diminishing personal value due to sexuality and/or gender identity. Working with this mode includes challenging schemas and maladaptive beliefs, as well as combating and disempowering prejudiced messages, promoting resilience factors, and reducing stress (Cardoso et al., 2022, 2024). This theoretical understanding guides the intervention, explaining the focus of the techniques in generating affirmation, pride, and in decreasing shame and dysfunctional internalizations (internalized thoughts and emotions stemming from an oppressive system).

Book Structure and Sequence of the PRISMAS Program Sessions

In the next chapters of this book, you will find a session-by-session guide of the PRISMAS intervention program. The chapters provide a detailed breakdown of the therapeutic sessions, showing practitioners how to conduct the intervention. The PRISMAS program consists of 12 sessions, which are detailed in the next chapters, organized into three parts.

The content of Chaps. 2–6, included in the first part of the book, is summarized in Table 1.2, which describes the initial sessions of the program (sessions 1 to 5).

Table 1.2 Initial sessions: Understanding Schema Therapy and my internal way of functioning

Session name	Main goals	Brief explanation
Session 1. "Connecting with my network and understanding my way of functioning"	Presentation of the group structure and key concepts of ST, establishing the foundations for the therapeutic program and creating a safe and supportive environment	The first session is psychoeducational and encourages self-monitoring by introducing the fundamental concepts of ST, addressing cognitions, emotions, sensations, behaviors, and modes. It establishes the foundations for the therapeutic program, with activities that promote the creation of secure bonds and connection between participants and therapists
Session 2. "Getting to know my different sides"	Creating a bond between participants and therapists and didactically introducing the understanding of the various schema modes	This meeting aims to solidify the participant–therapist bond. The different modes are thoroughly explored and organized, with the introduction of a mode map to guide future activities. Participants are assisted in identifying their ways of functioning
Session 3. "How society influenced the criticisms I internalized about myself"	Introduction to understanding how minority stress and stigma can cause suffering for SGM and how this issue can be addressed through ST and affirmative therapy	The third session aims to explore the interaction between social and cultural issues and the internalized stressors experienced by participants. In this way, the connection between personal suffering and the problems present in the surrounding society is gradually understood, encouraging the incorporation of new perspectives
Session 4. "Knowing and highlighting my strengths"	Identification of the healthy adult mode and personal strengths, in conjunction with the strengthening of this mode	In the fourth session, the focus is on strengthening the affirmative healthy adult mode through practical and thematic exercises therapists assist participants in identifying the stimuli that activate this mode, allowing them to recognize their strengths and areas for development. The session takes place in a welcoming environment, which celebrates sexual diversity and challenges cisheteronormative culture
Session 5. "Connecting with my history"	Strengthening of the healthy adult mode, preparing participants for future interventions that are emotionally deeper	The fifth session solidifies initial learnings and deepens understanding of the healthy adult mode, offering self-care tools additionally, it includes an activity aimed at combating the inner critic (oppressive sociocultural) mode, preparing participants for the next stage of the intervention

The content of Chaps. 7–11, included in the second part of the book, is summarized in Table 1.3, which describes the intermediate sessions of the program (sessions 6 to 10).

Finally, the content of Chaps. 12 and 13, included in the third part of the book, is summarized in Table 1.4, which describes the final sessions of the program (sessions 11 and 12).

Table 1.3 Intermediate sessions: Changing my way of thinking, acting, and feeling through the integration of Schema Therapy and Affirmative Therapy

Session name	Main goals	Brief explanation
Session 6. "I think, therefore I (do not) criticize myself"	Development of important skills to deal with thoughts linked to the inner critic (oppressive sociocultural) mode	This session aims to help participants identify cognitive patterns associated with the inner critic (oppressive sociocultural) mode through self-monitoring, followed by the application of cognitive restructuring techniques
Session 7. "The child who lives in me"	This is an intercalary meeting between sessions aimed at disempowering the inner critic (oppressive sociocultural) mode the goal is to welcome child modes and provide a secure base that subsequently allows participants to pursue deep emotional change	In this session, child modes are explored and explained in more detail. Experiential techniques are used to enhance participants' connection to the experiences associated with these modes and their individual life stories
Session 8. "Where does this internal storm come from? Understanding my emotions"	Identifying various emotions and how they are associated with different modes this recognition is necessary for later exploring emotionally activating situations with greater care and sensitivity	The session includes exercises aimed at the perception and labeling of emotions in a playful and interactive manner. Thus, participants are placed in a welcoming space for emotional exploration, without, however, addressing potentially more triggering aspects
Session 9. "Allowing myself a new way of feeling"	The focus is on emotional regulation, with the goal of promoting deeper emotional change by exploring significant life experiences that may be associated with the inner critic (oppressive sociocultural) mode	To achieve the goal of deepening the process and facilitating emotional transformation, therapists use chairwork and imagery exercises in this meeting
Session 10. "Acting as the person I aspire to be"	Identifying and encouraging healthy coping strategies. This aims to promote flexibility and the ability to manage dysfunctional strategies used to handle difficulties	This session aims to promote behavioral changes related to the inner critic (oppressive sociocultural) mode. To achieve this goal, various strategies are employed, including assertiveness training, role-playing, and therapeutic writing. Coping modes are also reviewed and discussed

Table 1.4 Final sessions: Solidifying and strengthening my affirmative healthy adult and having fun with my happy child

Session name	Main goals	Brief explanation
Session 11. "Connecting our individual strengths to health and affirmation"	Strengthening of the affirmative healthy Adult mode, connected to the social group, focusing on the acceptance of gender identity and/or sexual orientation and the formation of healthy relationships	In this session, interventions focused on strengthening participants' self-acceptance of sexual orientation and/or gender identity, promoting connection with positive examples from the LGBTQIA+ community, and developing healthy relationships. This is achieved through the repetition of the safe place technique, with emphasis on acceptance of one's own sexuality and identity, by introducing and applying the concept of "schema chemistry" to understand how life history influences relational choices, and by creating models of healthier relationships, encouraging mutual respect, open communication, and autonomy
Session 12. "Releasing the happy child"	Emotional and creative expression of participants, allowing them to release worries and stresses, cultivating joy and play, and sharing their experiences in the group, celebrating the established connections	In the closing session, therapists guide therapeutic activities that allow participants to express their emotions, share their experiences in the group, and say goodbye in a positive way. Participants imagine themselves leaving behind worries and stresses. Then, they share their symbolic creations related to the group experiences. There is emphasis on the importance of the work done and encouragement for the application of the learnings in everyday life

References

Arntz, A., Rijkeboer, M., Chan, E., Fassbinder, E., Karaosmanoglu, A., Lee, C. W., & Panzeri, M. (2021). Towards a reformulated theory underlying schema therapy: Position paper of an international workgroup. *Cognitive Therapy and Research, 45*, 1007–1020. https://doi.org/10.1007/s10608-021-10209-5

Bach, B., Lockwood, G., & Young, J. E. (2017). A new look at the schema therapy model: Organization and role of early maladaptive schemas. *Cognitive Behaviour Therapy, 47*(4), 328–349. https://doi.org/10.1080/16506073.2017.1410566

Beck, A. T. (1976). *Cognitive therapy and the emotional disorders*. Penguin Books.

Cardoso, B. L. A., & Campos, J. G. F. (2023). Luca e o modo crítico (sociocultural opressor) internalizado: contribuições da terapia do esquema para intervenção com minorias sociais. In B. L. A. Cardoso & K. Paim (Eds.), *Terapia do esquema no cinema: os filmes e séries na compreensão da prática clínica* (pp. 337–360). Artesã.

Cardoso, B. L. A., Paim, K., Catelan, R. F., & Liebross, E. H. (2022). Minority stress and the inner critic/oppressive sociocultural schema mode among sexual and gender minorities. *Current Psychology, 42*, 19991–19999. https://doi.org/10.1007/s12144-022-03086-y

Cardoso, B. L. A., Lima, A. F. A., Costa, F. R. M., Loose, C., Liu, X., & Fabris, M. A. (2024). Sociocultural implications in the development of early maladaptive schemas in adolescents belonging to sexual and gender minorities. *International Journal of Environmental Research and Public Health, 21*(8). https://doi.org/10.3390/ijerph21080971

Costa, P. T., & McCrae, R. R. (1992). *NEO personality inventory-revised (NEO-PI-R) and NEO five-factor inventory (NEO-FFI) professional manual.* Psychological Assessment Resources.

Paim, K., Cardoso, B. L. A., Algarves, C. P., & Behary, W. (2020). Bases Teóricas e Aplicação da Terapia do Esquema para Casais. In B. L. A. Cardoso & K. Paim (Eds.), *Terapias Cognitivo-Comportamentais para casais e famílias: Bases teóricas, pesquisas e intervenções* (p. 79). Sinopsys.

Papalia, D. E., & Feldman, R. D. (2011). *Human development* (12th ed.). McGraw-Hill.

Piaget, J. (1952). *The origins of intelligence in children* (M. Cook, Trans.). International Universities Press. (Original work published 1936).

Rafaeli, E., Bernstein, D. P., & Young, J. (2011). *Schema therapy.* Routledge.

Young, J. E., Klosko, J. S., & Weishaar, M. E. (2003). *Schema therapy: A practitioner's guide.* Guilford Press.

Part I
Initial Sessions: Understanding Schema Therapy and My Internal Way of Functioning

Chapter 2
"Connecting with My Network and Understanding My Way of Functioning": Bond Creation and Self-monitoring

The first session of this manual focuses on the introduction to the theoretical basis of ST, presenting concepts such as cognitions, emotions, sensations, behaviors, and the general concept of modes in a didactic and playful way. The initial session is designed to establish the necessary foundations for the application of the therapeutic program. Initial experiential activities are also carried out aimed at creating a safe environment of support and mutual understanding among the group members. The focus is on establishing bonds and connection between the participants and therapists, along with the beginning of psychoeducation and self-monitoring (Table 2.1).

Group Presentation

Objectives: To create the initial bond between the group; present the structure and content that will be used during the program.

Procedure: The therapist welcomes the group, thanking the participants for their taking part and presence at that meeting. They introduce themselves, saying their name, telling a little about their training, and sharing a piece of personal information, thereby creating a more intimate first moment of contact. Then, the therapist asks the rest of the group to introduce themselves, repeating the same idea: saying their name, their age, and a personal fact about themselves. The co-therapist is the last to introduce themself, closing the cycle and returning the word to the therapist. Both of the therapists then present, in a summarized and concise way, the general idea of how the group will work and the basic schedule of the sessions (which will also be received by the participants, in a physical folder). The ideal is just to quickly point out the structure and planning of the meetings, to create a sense of organization and stability, without spending too much time going into details at this time.

B. L. A. Cardoso, A. C. G. Braga, *The PRISMAS Group Therapy Handbook*,
https://doi.org/10.1007/978-3-031-91809-4_2

Table 2.1 Session activities and estimated duration

Activity/Intervention	Estimated duration
Group presentation	25 min
Brief presentation of the concept of modes	30 min
Initial imagery exercise: Safe place technique	20 min
Group agreements and rules	15 min
Yarn/string technique	20 min
Feedback and action plan	10 min

Application tips: For forming a closer group bond, it is important that a true fact about oneself is expressed, but being careful not to break the limits of the therapeutic relationship. This suggestion applies to all self-disclosure present during the program. Also, it may be interesting to suggest that the curiosity about oneself goes beyond the issues of work or studies, since the affirmative healthy adult has already attained the construction of a strengthened and authentic sense of identity (e.g., "I really like superhero movies and I've seen all the Marvel movies," "I'm a fashion fan and I love personal coloring"). This can be a first chance for participants to see themselves in a broad way, beyond just the work and academic functions. This helps to create the rhythm of the intervention, with the therapists' posture always serving as a healthy model. Finally, the co-therapist in this activity needs to be attentive to the reactions of the participants, noting if any emotional reactivity or avoidance during the experience arises—potentially indicating behavior they will repeat during all the next meetings. It is also suggested for both therapists to give positive feedback, verbally ("how interesting, *participants' name*!" "and how was that, *participants' name?*") and non-verbally (smiling, nodding, listening attentively) to the participants' responses, creating a sense of security within the group. All these tips apply to the various interventions in the manual.

Brief Presentation of the Concept of Modes

Objectives: To introduce the concept of modes; address initial expectations of participants with the group; help create a sense of self-monitoring that will be better explored in the next sessions.

Procedure: The therapists start with the following questions: "What thoughts went through your head when you decided to participate in the group? How are you feeling in this first meeting? Did you notice any different sensation in your body when you came here today?" Then, they let each participant answer about their thoughts, feelings, and sensations regarding participation. It is helpful to name along with them the cognitions, emotions, and sensory experience, subtly instructing self-monitoring. For example: In response to a member who said they had noticed their heart racing when passing through the door and experiencing racing thoughts due to the fear of not being a good enough participant or not being able to meet the group's schedule, the therapist might say: "Oh, so you had thoughts about your fear of not being good enough and you were experiencing anxiety, feeling it through your accelerated heart rate?" helping that person to classify their internal processes. It is also worth welcoming them, establishing an atmosphere of limited reparenting, an essential process of ST. Continuing the example: "Thank you for sharing this with us. It's brave of you to talk about these fears. I'm sure many people would feel the same way when starting something new. I'm glad that, despite this, you are here with us!" The focus here is not to question thoughts or work on emotions deeply. This will be the goal of the later sessions of this program. At first, in short, it is enough to maintain curiosity and clarity to name processes and adopt the posture of a good caregiver when welcoming the participants' emotions.

Therapists can proceed by asking about behaviors. "Did anyone here feel like missing the meeting? Or did you get so excited that you started reading about ST even before we met?" In the face of the participants' responses, they can maintain the same caregiving attitude that was held for the previous questions. They can use the participants' responses to continue the exercise, highlighting the different ways people function. For example: "Guys, did you notice that some of you were excited and happy to be here, while others were anxious and worried? There were even people who felt irritated because they had to wake up early in the morning to meet with us. We are not going to judge any of these perceptions. All of them are valid! What we want with this exercise is just to show that we all have different ways of functioning. I'm sure that whoever was feeling afraid doesn't feel frightened all the time, just as whoever is happy has their own angry moments. Can anyone share with us about a moment this week when they felt, thought or acted differently from the way they are feeling now here today?"

From this, the therapists can introduce the concept of schema modes, that is, the various parts that each person has within themselves that appear more or less strongly in the face of different situations. Therapists can ask for examples of thoughts and emotions that arose when different "parts" of each one were present. For example: "*Participants' name*, you said that today you were happy and excited to be in a group with people similar to you, but when you tried to do individual therapy, you became anxious, ended up giving up and made up an excuse to pause the process. Can you tell me, if you feel comfortable, what thoughts went through your head when this side of you that wanted to run away came up? Did you feel any kind of different sensation in your body? What is different about this happy and excited side of today?" The focus here is to try to get responses exemplifying the different modes that each participant experiences.

Initially, it is not necessary to categorize them yet. In order for them to absorb the information progressively and understand the concept of modes in their lives in a practical way, this session seeks only to initiate the process of self-monitoring, through psychoeducation about the existence of modes and what they are.

The explanation of what a mode is can be summarized as follows: schema modes are simultaneous activations of emotions, memories, cognitions, and behaviors (Louis et al., 2018; Young et al., 2003) that can arise in response to the nurturing or lack thereof of our emotional needs. They have their origins in our life history, especially in childhood, and continue to influence the way the person relates to themselves and the world around them. When a mode is activated, a person can have impulsive and emotionally guided reactions, different from the ones they usually would have. Some modes can be more easily identified by bringing specific reactions to the body and mind (e.g., growing hot in the face, loud and accelerated thoughts, and intense anger when in the angry child).

In the therapeutic group, the goal is to identify these modes, understand their origins and patterns, and then work to regulate them in a healthier and more balanced way. By recognizing and welcoming these different internal parts, the person can develop a greater connection with themselves and a deeper understanding of their emotional needs, which contributes to a positive transformation and better overall well-being. The objective is not to stop being who you are, but to understand your different parts, strengthen what is healthy, and learn to effectively use your various sides.

After presenting this concept in an accessible way and appropriate to the level of understanding of that group, therapists can open the discussion again, asking things like: "In what situations have you noticed different 'parts' of you appearing? Have you ever looked back, after experiencing an intense emotion and thought 'why did I do that? That doesn't seem like me'? If so, do you have an example of when that happened? Can you connect any of these parts with your life stories?"

Application tips: It is interesting to encourage everyone to participate and take care that more talkative group members do not completely dominate the conversation, nor more avoidant members stay silent all the time. Understanding each person's dynamics and encouraging connection and exchange is one of the most important functions of the co-therapist. Still, participants should not be pressured to speak if it activates them emotionally. Similarly, if the co-therapist notices any kind of discomfort and dysregulation in one of the participants, they can call them over privately and provide quick support, without exposing them (e.g., asking if they want to get a drink of water and going along). If the group as a whole is more inhibited, therapists can initially bring more hypothetical examples to complete the reasoning of the activity, reinforcing the responses received and encouraging everyone to share their stories, reminding them that this is a safe place and they can feel free from judgments there, offering a lot of support. If the majority are talkative and the activities extend far beyond the estimated time, organizing the order of who speaks, assertively preventing intrusions into colleagues' sharing and offering affective limits when necessary becomes part of the therapeutic focus.

Initial Imagery Exercise: Safe Place Technique

Objectives: To start preparing the group for future experiential techniques; introduce emotional regulation skills and tools.

Procedure: After the completion of the presentation exercise, the main therapist introduces the notion that, throughout the sessions, several experiential activities will be carried out that can help participants connect better with their emotions, understand them, and accept them. This facilitates knowing and guiding each of the various parts that make up each person in the most useful and healthy way for each of them. The therapist asks if everyone would feel comfortable trying out the first exercise. The therapist or co-therapist explains what a safe place imagery is—it is a space where the person feels good and comfortable in all senses. The space, visually, should remind them of shelter. The sounds and smells are pleasant and calming. It can be a place that exists, existed, or that was simply imagined by the participant. They can describe how it is expected that not everyone will have a place like this in mind instantly. In this case, it is possible to create an imaginary place. The therapist or co-therapist can give a quick example of real or hypothetical safe places for them (e.g., a bedroom, someone special's house, a forest, a beach), helping in understanding the exercise by the individuals of the group. For a better understanding of imagery techniques, intervention implementers can access van der Wijngaart (2021).

Narration of the activity: "*Close your eyes or keep looking down, if it's more comfortable for you at the moment. Initially focus your attention on your breathing, letting it slow down. (Pause). When we breathe slowly, our brain understands that it's time to relax, which facilitates the feeling of being safe, which is what we want with this exercise. (Pause). If you notice that you are tensing any part of your body, release it. Release your jaw, if you notice there's tension. Lower the tongue from the roof of your mouth. Let your forehead, back and eyebrows relax. (Pause). If thoughts arise during the exercise, that's okay. You can gently let go of them and focus again on the image being described. (Pause). Now, gradually, let the image of a place where you feel protected, a place that makes you feel calm, comfortable and secure, come to mind. Imagine the details of this environment, the colors that compose it. See if you can perceive the textures of this place, the objects that are present, what the lighting is like. Allow yourself to spend some time observing and absorbing the scenario. (Pause). Now try to notice the sounds. What kind of music or noises can you perceive in this place? Let those sounds help you feel calm and quiet. (Pause). Now, notice if there are any smells that relax you, too. What does the place you are imagining smell like? (Pause). Try to be there, attentive to all your senses. Choose to invite someone or some being (like an animal or teddy bear) to be with you in this image. Who did you bring to the scene? It is important that the guest makes you feel good and is a welcoming company. (Pause). Stay for a few minutes living this scene, knowing that you can always return to it if you need comfort and support. (Pause). Now, gradually, let the scene darken and focus again on your breathing. Breathe as slowly and deeply as you can. (Pause). Give small movements to your body, for example, moving your neck or stretching. When you're ready, open your eyes, ending the practice.*"

Application tips: The most important thing in this exercise is to introduce the idea of imagery. Although a verbal explanation is important, it is in the experience that the transformative potential lies. It is ideal to not talk too much on how the practice works, emphasizing instead to participants to actually try the safe place technique, rather than just talking about it. If the co-therapist or therapist notices any agitation or discomfort from a participant, they can address this after the completion of the activity, using this learning opportunity to explain the internal processes that happen in an imagery exercise (avoidance, resistance, etc.), after welcoming that person. It is worth emphasizing the importance of the narration being slow, with a calm and paused voice, respecting the time of formulation of the image. The rhythm of the narration guides much of the internal experience of the person who is receiving the intervention. Speeding up too much can have the opposite effect of the desired outcomes, generating stress.

It is important to read and practice the exercise beforehand, so that it becomes more authentic and expressive, intentionally passing the emotion of calm and serenity. It is advisable to avoid reading the practice directly, although it is feasible to use a paper guide to help remember the order of speeches, as long as you do not depend on it.

Agreements and Group Rules (Summary Form Also Received by Participants)

Objectives: To establish clear agreements and rules that will guide the therapeutic process; promote an atmosphere of safety, respect, and empathy, allowing all participants to feel welcomed and comfortable; formulate agreements together, aiming to increase the engagement and sense of belonging.

Procedure: For this task, each participant will receive a blank sheet of paper, where they will write the agreements. Thus, they can keep them and take them home. The objective is that this is a joint construction, so the therapists can start by asking for suggestions from members about what would make them feel more comfortable, safe, and engaged among the group. They can ask about each person's fears and expectations to prevent possible misunderstandings or frustrations. Some important agreements, if not mentioned by anyone, include:

Confidentiality and secrecy: Everything shared in the group is strictly confidential. What is said in the therapeutic space stays in the therapeutic space. This ensures a safe environment for the genuine expression of feelings.

Respect: It is essential to respect each participant's speech, without interruptions or judgments. Everyone has the right to express their thoughts and feelings freely and without embarrassment. For this, organization of discussions and talking order is necessary.

Active listening: The practice of active listening is encouraged during sessions. This means that each participant will strive to listen with empathy and understanding, showing genuine interest in the experiences and life stories of others.

Self-responsibility and commitment: Each participant is responsible for their actions and reactions in the group. We encourage reflection on how their behaviors can affect themselves, others, and the therapeutic environment as a whole. For example, this includes the need to arrive on time, do homework, and actively participate in activities.

Application tips: The idea of agreements is close to that of a therapeutic contract. The clearer everyone is about what promotes a good environment and good relationships, the better the experience will be. It is important to have clear and accessible boundaries for everyone, as well as presence, constancy, and security on the part of the therapists, who should adhere to all rules and serve as a model for the participants. Each group will bring authentic suggestions, and they should be understood and respected by the therapists. These agreements can be revisited at other times, helping to establish responsibility among the participants. If used appropriately, they can be a great tool for reparenting by providing predictability and healthy boundaries.

Yarn/String Technique

Objectives: To bring group participants closer; visualize interpersonal relationships in the group context.

Procedure: Participants are instructed to form a circle (if they are not already seated in this format), so that everyone can see and interact easily. The activity begins with one of the participants holding the beginning of the yarn/string in their hands. This participant is encouraged to share something personal or an emotion related to the experiences lived during the first day of interventions (e.g., an emotion that arose during the safe place technique or what they think of having colleagues with similar experiences nearby). After sharing, this participant throws the ball to another person in the group, keeping the end of the thread in their hands. One suggestion is for one of the therapists to start the activity, to serve as a model for the others, saying, for example, how it is for them to guide the group and what they thought of being in contact with everyone. It is suggested to try to be motivating, saying something like: "after so much preparation, I am very happy to see the group happening. I was anxious at the beginning, but now I feel closer to you and confident." Despite this, it is important to remain genuine and say only what you really feel. This also applies to the participants. It is important to explain that they can be honest, without feeling obliged to say something positive if they do not feel that way.

The next person who receives the ball should hold the piece of yarn that was thrown to them and then share something that is related to what was previously shared. After sharing their story, this person passes the ball, without letting go of their piece, to another person in the group, creating a visual connection between the participants. The process continues, with each participant sharing and passing the ball to another member, until everyone has had the opportunity to speak and connect to the ball.

At the end of the activity, the group will have formed a web of connections with the yarn/string, representing the relationships and interactions between the participants. At this point, it is possible to visually observe how the experiences, emotions, and stories shared are intertwined, showing the importance of emotional connection between group members. A brief reflection on the activity is conducted, highlighting this visual aspect and encouraging participants to share their perceptions about the web formed.

This activity helps to create a sense of cohesion and belonging in the group, as well as promoting active listening and empathy among the participants. The visualization of the connections can enhance this experience. At the end of the activity, each one cuts a piece of the yarn to take with them for the duration of the group—whether tying it as a ring, keeping it in their wallet, or attaching it to a keychain, for example. It symbolizes the bond between those present.

Application tips: It is highly recommended that therapists keep this thread as an emotional object. It is a way to feel connected to the participants during the week, remind them of the connection with the group, and show them that they care about the therapeutic process. Bringing it during the meetings can be a way to subtly encourage the idea that they are there and are also part of that group.

Feedback and Action Plan

Before ending the meeting, the therapists ask for feedback from the participants about the interventions carried out. They ask how they felt about the proposed activities, whether they found them useful for better understanding the concepts addressed, and whether any part of the intervention generated insecurity or doubt. The therapists emphasize that the participants' perceptions and opinions are valuable for adjusting the therapeutic work according to the needs of the group, encouraging them to share their experiences and impressions of what they experienced in the session.

It is explained that each participant will receive a folder or envelope to store materials that will be handed out during the meetings. The group's agreements, which were drafted on the first day, can already be placed in the folder. The therapists also explain that, at each session, an action plan for the week will be received, allowing them to practice what was worked on there outside of the therapeutic environment. This is a way to maintain and strengthen the gains from that therapeutic process. They make themselves available to support them in their reflections and clarify any doubts that may arise during the implementation of the action plan (it is suggested to create a group on a social network platform that can facilitate communication and sending messages). It is requested that they bring a childhood photo for an activity that will be carried out at the beginning of the next session.

Action plan: Continue to perceive during the week how your thoughts, emotions, sensations, and behaviors are connected to the modes; bring a childhood photo to the next meeting.

Appendices and materials needed for Session 1
– List with the names of the group participants
– Specific group manual, containing the basic schedule of the sessions and information about the structure and operation
– Group rules form

References

Louis, J. P., Wood, A. M., Lockwood, G., Ho, M. R., & Ferguson, E. (2018). Positive clinical psychology and schema therapy (ST): The development of the Young positive schema questionnaire (YPSQ) to complement the Young schema questionnaire 3 short form (YSQ-S3). *Psychological Assessment, 30*(9), 1199–1213. https://doi.org/10.1037/pas0000567

van der Wijngaart, R. (2021). *Imagery rescripting: Theory and practice*. Pavilion Publishing & Media.

Young, J. E., Klosko, J. S., & Weishaar, M. E. (2003). *Schema therapy: A practitioner's guide*. Guilford Press.

Further Reading

Cardoso, B. L. A., Lima, A. F. A., Costa, F. R. M., Loose, C., Liu, X., & Fabris, M. A. (2024). Sociocultural implications in the development of early maladaptive schemas in adolescents belonging to sexual and gender minorities. *International Journal of Environmental Research and Public Health, 21*(8). https://doi.org/10.3390/ijerph21080971

Cardoso, B. L. A., Paim, K., Catelan, R. F., & Liebross, E. H. (2022). Minority stress and the inner critic/oppressive sociocultural schema mode among sexual and gender minorities. *Current Psychology, 42*, 19991–19999. https://doi.org/10.1007/s12144-022-03086-y

Farrell, J. M., & Shaw, I. A. (2012). *Group schema therapy for borderline personality disorder: A step-by-step treatment manual with patient workbook*. Wiley-Blackwell.

Farrell, J. M., & Shaw, I. A. (2020). Creative use of mode dialogues with the vulnerable child and dysfunctional critic modes. In J. S. Heath & M. Startup (Eds.), *Creative methods in schema therapy: Advances and innovation in clinical practice*. Routledge.

Rafaeli, E., Bernstein, D. P., & Young, J. (2011). *Schema therapy*. Routledge.

Chapter 3
"Getting to Know my Different Sides": Presentation of Modes

In the second session, the different schema modes are addressed. The participants are introduced to the mode map, which will guide them in the activities of the upcoming sessions. The meeting aims to deepen the identification of their own modes, with special emphasis on the inner critic (oppressive sociocultural) mode and the affirmative healthy adult mode. Therapists use practical techniques, such as imagery, to help group members explore and understand these ways of functioning, which will be better worked on in the following sessions (Table 3.1).

Connection with the Vulnerable Child: Childhood Photo Technique

Objectives: To connect participants with their own emotional needs and explore, in a practical way, the presence of a mode and the reactions and activations related to it.

Procedure: The therapists start the session by asking about the participants' week and introducing an "ice-breaker" topic to start the dialogue. After this moment, they introduce the first activity. They remind the participants of the childhood photo requested at the end of the previous meeting and ask them to get it, either physically or on their cell phone. If someone does not have access to the image, the therapists ask the participant to imagine themselves during that period, trying to remember how they dressed and what they looked like.

Activity narration: "*I ask that, now, you take the photo that we agreed on last week. You can look at it on your cell phone or, if you have brought a printout, at that. Start by taking deep breaths five times. (Pause). Then, try to connect with this child version of you. How old are you in this photo? What is your life and your routine like? Generally, how do you feel? Answer these questions in your head. (Pause). Take a few deep breaths and now observe the details of the image. How are you dressed? What was your appearance and your personality like? (Pause). Close your*

B. L. A. Cardoso, A. C. G. Braga, *The PRISMAS Group Therapy Handbook*,
https://doi.org/10.1007/978-3-031-91809-4_3

Table 3.1 Session activities and estimated duration

Activity/Intervention	Estimated duration
Connection with the vulnerable child—Childhood photo technique	30 min
Review of the action plan	15 min
Presentation of the mode map	45 min
Bubble technique	20 min
Feedback and action plan	10 min

eyes and try to feel as if you were that child again. Bring the image to mind as vividly and detailed as you can. (Pause). Now, try to remember the happy moments, the difficult moments, and the challenges that this child faced. (Pause). Answer to yourself, calmly, the following question, still with your eyes closed: 'what do you need in that photo/moment?'. (Pause). How do you feel? Answer internally. (Pause). Try to imagine this need being met, you receiving what you need. (Pause). How do you feel? (Pause). Take a few more deep breaths. Give small movements to your arms, legs, and neck, and let the image fade. (Pause). When you feel ready, open your eyes."

After the narration, the therapists ask the participants to describe their experience. The focus here is the connection with their own child and what this brought in terms of thoughts, sensations, emotions, and behaviors. At this moment, it is not necessary to intervene or delve into the contents brought up by the group members—the objective is just to start identifying the child modes, mainly the vulnerable child.

Application tips: The therapists, when narrating the activity, should speak directly to the child, as if they were talking to the child side of the patients. Instead of asking "how do they feel in this routine?" it is more therapeutic to say, "how do you feel in this routine?" This helps the person connect with the narrated image, creating an emotional closeness.

Review of the Action Plan

After the first activity, the therapists conduct a quick review of the previous action plan, related to the attempt to perceive the different modes they were in throughout the week. They start by briefly reminding the exercise, which consisted of each participant identifying their different ways of being, from activating situations, thoughts, emotions, and behaviors.

The therapists ask the participants if they had any difficulty or if they wish to share something they discovered about themselves during the task. This is an opportunity for participants to bring their own experiences and insights on how the different modes manifest in their lives. They can also ask about the first activity, linked to the child modes. It is possible to question aspects such as: "What did you notice differently when connecting with your child? What did you feel in the exercise we did? Do you remember other situations throughout life where you felt this way?"

This quick review not only serves to emphasize the concepts learned earlier, but also helps to establish continuity and cohesion in the group's therapeutic work, keeping everyone on the same page and engaged in the process. This review will be carried out at all meetings.

Presentation of the Mode Map

Objectives: To use the experiences and reports of participants about their week as a starting point to build a schema mode map; identify the different modes that make up human experience.

Procedure: Therapists can start this activity from the group's reports on the modes identified during the week. Therapists can organize and classify the examples of thoughts and emotions that arose when different "parts" of each one were present. For example: "Jack, you said you were anxious and wanted to make up an excuse not to come to the meeting, but ended up deciding to participate. Can you tell me, if you feel comfortable, what thoughts went through your head when this side of you that wanted to run away came up? Did you feel any different sensation in your body?" The focus is to obtain examples of coping modes, child modes (vulnerable, angry, undisciplined and happy), inner critic modes (including the oppressive sociocultural), and the healthy adult mode. If these examples do not arise spontaneously, therapists can give personal examples (always respecting therapeutic boundaries) or bring hypothetical situations.

The main focus of the intervention is the strengthening of the affirmative healthy adult and the combat of the inner critic (oppressive sociocultural) mode. The other modes, such as the vulnerable and happy child and the coping modes, will also be addressed in some sessions. It is important that participants absorb as much information as possible about all these key concepts of the program. This is a long activity and essential for the proper functioning of the rest of the program; therefore, it is recommended to use most of the meeting time on it.

Therapists explain that, during PRISMAS, it is expected to identify these modes, understand their origins and patterns, and then work to regulate them in a healthier and more balanced way. By recognizing and welcoming these different parts of oneself, a person can develop a greater connection with oneself and a deeper understanding of their emotional needs, which contributes to a positive transformation and better overall well-being. It is not necessary to stop being who you are, but to understand your different parts, strengthen what is healthy, and learn to effectively use your various sides, also taking care of the challenging parts. Below, the explanations of each mode that is addressed in the intervention according to the definitions of Cardoso et al. (2022), Farrell and Shaw (2018), Wainer and Rijo (2016), and Young et al. (2003) will be presented. Illustrations, drawings, and psychoeducational cards can be used as a visual resource to exemplify different schematic modes for the group participants.

Child Modes

Vulnerable child mode: The vulnerable child mode is characterized by the inner part that carries the memories and emotions related to painful events or experiences lived in childhood. Therapists can emphasize that it was with this part that participants connected in the photography exercise. When activated, this mode can bring up feelings of fear, insecurity, helplessness, and sadness. The person, in this mode, appears more fragile and in search of comfort. The vulnerable child tends to seek protection and security from others, yearning for care and validation. In this state, the person may sometimes feel excluded, rejected, and in danger in relationships, which generates insecurity in connection and bonding. They can express emotions and needs in a direct and emotional way. Physically, a person in this mode may have sensations such as anguish, nauseous, and accelerated breathing, with facial expressions of insecurity or sadness. They may withdraw and verbalize their difficulties and vulnerabilities. It is a very primary and emotional mode, which communicates the need for comfort and security, as well as autonomy and self-esteem.

Undisciplined/impulsive child mode: The undisciplined child is characterized by a resistance to discipline and rules. This inner part can manifest as a reaction of rebellion or contempt for established norms. This mode may be associated with experiences of restriction or excessive control in childhood—or, on the contrary, lack of limits, leading to the desire to break the imposed barriers. This behavior, however, is impulsive and unmeasured, without deep reflection. The person in this mode acts in a self-focused way, guided by primary emotions, seeking to feel safe and supplied in relationships through hasty behaviors, often putting themselves and others in unwanted situations. This mode can manifest as difficulty in waiting for long-term rewards, preferring immediate pleasures, similar to a spoiled child, with little resistance to boredom and frustration. The undisciplined child can be impulsive and challenging, but deep down seeks affective and healthy limits.

Angry child mode: The angry child mode is characterized by an inner part that harbors intense and natural emotions of anger and frustration. This mode may have been influenced by experiences of injustice, lack of limits, or even emotional abuses in childhood. The child, when expressing intense emotions, seeks to supply what it believes has been curtailed, trying to correct what it perceives as injustices, as a form of self-protection. When activated, the angry child can manifest through emotional outbursts, unexpected reactions, and aggressive behaviors, with anger being directed both at oneself and others, and sometimes even at objects. It is important to note that anger in this mode shows, albeit inappropriately, the non-fulfillment of a core emotional need (e.g., "Nobody pays attention to me!"). The focus of the intervention is not to suppress anger, but to seek an assertive way to express it to ensure that needs are met. Here we differentiate the anger of emotional frustration, typical of the child mode, from the anger of attack (as in "You are no good!" or "You are useless"), which characterizes more the coping modes (explained later in this manual). Common physical sensations in this mode include heat, redness in the cheeks, sweat, louder and more imposing speech, and facial expressions like tense eyebrows and lips. The emotional need is for validation and a safe environment in which to express and process their emotions.

Happy child mode: The happy child mode is characterized by internal light and joyful part, carrying memories of positive moments and well-being in childhood. This mode evokes feelings of joy, curiosity, creativity, and spontaneity, finding pleasure in the simplest activities and actively seeking games and forms of entertainment. A person in this mode may smile and laugh frequently, feeling pleasure and jubilation. This internal mode can be neglected or repressed by more serious modes or by the demands of adult life. Recognizing and valuing the happy child is essential to cultivating the ability to enjoy moments of contentment and to encourage fun and leisure, which are basic needs for emotional balance. In adult life, these joys often get sidelined due to work or academic responsibilities; however, it is very beneficial to bring these elements of childhood into adult life.

Inner Critic Modes

The inner critic modes are characterized by parts that internalized critical, punitive, and/or guilt-inducing messages stemming from other people (e.g., parents, uncles, grandparents, teachers) throughout development or from a broad and diffuse context (like culture). Over time, it is common for this mode to transform into a relentless inner critic, with intense thoughts that cause suffering (Farrell & Shaw, 2018).

The focus of PRISMAS is to deepen the understanding of the sociocultural internalizations that sexual and gender minorities can make of their context. For this, Cardoso et al. (2022) proposed the understanding of the inner critic (oppressive sociocultural) mode, which will be described next.

Inner critic (oppressive sociocultural) mode: In the case of the inner critic (oppressive sociocultural) mode, the internalizations were mainly social and cultural oppressive, anti-LGBT messages. In this mode, a person focuses on negative beliefs about oneself, feeding self-deprecating thoughts and severe judgments about their gender identity and/or sexual orientation. When activated, it can lead to excessive self-demand, perfectionism, and self-criticism, weakening self-esteem and generating a negative view of oneself. The main difference of this mode from other inner critic modes is the focus on personal devaluation due to sexuality, with a distorted self-image that sees itself as inadequate, wrong, or defective. This mode carries a strong fear of rejection and social isolation, resulting from messages that portray a diverse sexual orientation and/or gender identity as something wrong and unacceptable. Working with the inner critic (oppressive sociocultural) mode involves challenging these negative beliefs, cultivating a more compassionate and empathetic attitude toward oneself and, in the specific case of the oppressive sociocultural, combating the internalized anti-LGBT messages, understanding and reducing the effects of minority stress. It is worth noting that, often, this mode can adopt the tone of voice or vocabulary similar to that of an oppressive figure or entity, even though it is not restricted to a single person (like a religious entity or social context).

Dysfunctional Coping Modes

Coping modes usually develop as strategies to deal with difficulties experienced in childhood, with behaviors aimed at protecting the person. Although they were useful adaptations in times of helplessness and lack of emotional needs supply, in adult life these modes often become dysfunctional.

Compliant surrender mode: The compliant surrender mode is characterized by a part that tends to easily submit to others, without expressing its own needs and desires. This mode often avoids taking a stand when something negative happens, preferring to focus on others' needs to avoid conflicts. This self-denial, however, can generate resentment and tension, which are suppressed in the name of maintaining peace. The person who is in this mode may remain silent in the face of offenses, allow their personal boundaries to be invaded, and tolerate abusive behaviors without complaining or taking a stand. When activated, the compliant surrenderer submits to the desires of others, ignoring their own needs. To manage this mode, it is important to develop strategies that allow an assertive expression of one's own boundaries.

Avoidant modes: The avoidant modes are characterized by attitudes of avoidance of potentially painful experiences, with the aim of avoiding difficult emotions. The detached protector mode manifests when the person emotionally disconnects from challenging or traumatic situations, avoiding emotional suffering or stressful stimuli. This disconnection can be expressed as existential emptiness, boredom, somatization, and depersonalization, among others. The self-soothing protector mode seeks an immediate relief of uncomfortable emotions through active avoidance. In this mode, the person may adopt behaviors such as overeating or drinking, using substances, self-harming, playing video games, compulsively shopping online, overworking, participating in gambling, engaging in risky activities, and having unprotected sex, seeking to escape from distress through immediate escapes. Those in this mode need new strategies to connect with their own emotions and have space to express them without fear. Compulsions and addictions derived from avoidance also need to be addressed, exploring their origins, the needs they cover, and long-term behavioral strategies to modify them.

Various authors indicate several forms of overcompensatory modes, including (a) self-aggrandizing, (b) bully and attack, (c) attention/approval seeking, (d) perfectionist overcontroller, and (e) conning and manipulative (Rafaeli et al., 2011; Trapp, 2024; Wainer & Rijo, 2016; Young et al., 2003). *Self-aggrandizing*: this mode is characterized by an attempt to self-exalt as a way to deal with unpleasant sensations or perceptions of oneself—such as insecurity and inadequacy. It involves behaviors in which the individual positions themselves as superior to others, demonstrating selfish, controlling, and/or abusive attitudes. People in this mode believe that common rules do not apply to them, demonstrating a grandiose behavior and disrespecting others' boundaries. Their conduct usually reflects arrogance and insensitivity, which can result in interpersonal conflicts. *Bully and Attack*: in this mode, the person often uses threats and intimidation to achieve their goals, assuming an authoritarian and competitive posture that is not appropriate for the context. The pursuit of control is carried out through forms of violence, whether psychological, moral, or other types. It is likely that this effort to exert dominance results in ignoring the needs and feelings of those around them, which can generate significant conflicts. The activation of this mode is often associated with a desire to avoid vulnerability or humiliation. *Attention and approval seeking*: individuals in this mode are excessively focused on obtaining validation or approval from others—they seek to be the center of attention and focus on relationships based on the status that another person has or what a relationship can offer. This includes aesthetic or social criteria. This behavior reflects an attempt to compensate for feelings of inferiority or rejection, seeking external approval to validate their self-esteem. Perfectionist *Overcontroller*: people in this mode present extreme and obsessive perfectionism, with an exaggerated focus on performance in order to avoid criticism. They become hypervigilant and super attentive to the attitudes and intentions of others, often suspecting something wrong or hostile. This rigid control, both over themselves and the environment, is a way to deal with feelings of helplessness or to cope with deep fears of rejection or failure. However, this hypervigilance leads to emotional exhaustion and can paradoxically generate emotional disconnection and distancing. *Conning/Manipulative*: This mode is characterized by attempts at excessive control through lies and manipulations aimed at achieving goals. The individual may play the victim to avoid negative consequences or shift blame to others. This strategy reflects a dysfunctional attempt to cope with feelings of insecurity or vulnerability, seeking to maintain the sensation of being on top or in control of the situation. This posture can compromise trust in interpersonal relationships and perpetuate conflicts.

Affirmative Healthy Adult Mode

The healthy adult mode is characterized by an internal part that maintains a realistic and balanced perspective, making decisions based on careful information and reflections. A person in this mode is capable of taking responsibility for their actions, taking care of their needs, and dealing assertively with life's challenges while maintaining the ability to be vulnerable and connect with others. The healthy adult balances emotions with reason, acting with wisdom and discernment. In therapy, strengthening this mode is essential to promote emotional self-regulation, self-confidence, and a healthier approach to dealing with everyday issues. In the case of the affirmative healthy adult, this mode also includes the internalization of positive messages about one's own sexuality and identity, empowering the person with positive beliefs about who they are and favoring a positive self-image. This version of the healthy adult, adapted for LGBTQIA+ people, highlights the importance of an affirmative stance to counterbalance the social stigma they are exposed to. In PRISMAS, the affirmative healthy adult is represented with the colors of the rainbow, a symbol of LGBTQIA+ pride. The variety of colors also represents the balance it seeks between its own emotions and the various parts of itself, not repressing them, but finding healthy ways to integrate them.

Therapists assist each group participant in identifying the moments when they experience these modes and noticing how they individually manifest. It is recommended to present images and figures to facilitate the practical and visual understanding of the modes. The introduction to the colors that represent each emotion can also be an interesting exercise, considering that this activity will be deepened in Session 8. This already allows creating a connection between the flows of interventions. The images will also be useful in the pot exercise, in Session 4.

With the information collected, the therapists present a visual map of the identified schema modes (a summary of each mode with its respective character). This map, which can be constructed from the descriptions available in Appendix I, will be given to the participants in loose sheets to file in their folders. The modes map can be a useful tool for group consultation, especially when they forget a mode or need help identifying a pattern of operation in everyday life, outside the session. In addition, it can serve as a guide for future experiential activities focused on the modes, reminding participants about the content worked on. At the end of the presentation of the map, therapists can highlight the importance of the group's collective work to create and maintain a safe space, where everyone can explore and get to know their modes without fear of judgments.

Application tips: To foster collaborative reasoning, a step-by-step recommendation is: (a) present the modes based on the initial responses and examples of participants, as they arise; (b) identify with them other moments when they experienced the described modes, bringing new concrete examples connected to their experiences; (c) help the group to describe how the modes influence their emotions, thoughts, and behaviors; and (d) introduce the modes that participants did not identified spontaneously, repeating the previous steps. An effective strategy is to ask questions connected to the characteristics of each mode. For example, when discussing the vulnerable child mode, the therapists can ask if the participants have ever felt insecure or helpless in certain situations, exploring how these feelings arose and how they reacted to them. Similarly, when addressing the undisciplined child mode, they can question about situations where members acted impulsively or procrastinated. In addition, using the group context, a discussion can be initiated about the different forms and intensities with which a mode presents itself, considering the various life stories and personalities of the participants.

Bubble Technique

Objectives: Based on Farrell and Shaw (2012), this exercise aims to continue providing the group with experiential experiences and introduce emotional regulation skills and tools.

Procedure: The therapist or co-therapist explains that the "bubble" is similar to the "safe place"—a space of safety, protection, and care that seeks to bring comfort to everyone. Visually, it is a welcoming environment with soft and pleasant colors. The purpose of this exercise is to welcome the various emotions that may have been awakened in the previous activities. Therapists can explain that child modes need welcoming without criticism, judgments, or avoidance, as they represent our most primary and essential emotions. Therefore, throughout the group, activities aimed at the child part of the participants will be carried out with kindness and care.

Activity narration: "Let's start the exercise by finding a comfortable position. Close your eyes or look down. Now, focus on your breathing. Breathe deeply, slowing down the pace. (Pause). Inhale 3 to 5 times, thinking that when inhaling you are taking in calm and tranquil energy, and when exhaling, release all the tension and stress from your body. (Pause).

Now, visualize a transparent and colorful bubble, a magical bubble that protects everyone in this room. Imagine that, at first, only you are inside it, sitting in your chair. The environment is calm, pleasant and quiet. Stay with this feeling of protection for a few moments. (Pause). After a few minutes, visualize the bubble expanding and sheltering one more person — it can be me or a colleague with whom you feel good. (Pause). Gradually, expand it until everyone is present. The bubble is big enough to shelter all of us here. (Pause). It has all the colors of the rainbow, with a soft and comforting glow. It also has a sweet and pleasant, light aroma. Feel how this bubble is powerful and unbreakable, a safe space where nothing bad can reach you. (Pause).

Inside this bubble, you can bring anything with you that brings you comfort and tranquility. It can be a special object, a dear memory or a significant place. Imagine bringing these good feelings and sensations inside. (Pause). Each of us is bringing a symbolic and significant object. I, for example, am bringing my [insert here the significant object of the therapist or co-therapist]. You don't need to say what yours is; just add it to your mental image. (Pause). No one can bring aggressive or pain-causing objects into the bubble, as it is a space of care. (Pause).

While we are in this bubble, nothing that happens outside it can affect us. It is like a protective shield that allows us to explore our emotions with serenity and peace. You are safe and protected. (Pause).

Stay in this scenario for a few minutes, experiencing the feeling of safety and comfort. Know that you can always return to this bubble when you need protection and refuge in difficult times — it is a special secret of our group. (Pause). Now, imagine that the bubble shrinks to the size of a marble. Put it in your pocket. In day-to-day life, it becomes invisible, but you can use it whenever you need. Only we, from the group, will know about its existence. (Pause).

Gradually, bring your attention back to your breathing. Breathe deeply, feeling your body relax even more. Inhale and exhale deeply three times. (Pause). When you feel ready, move your body lightly and open your eyes, bringing this feeling of tranquility to the present moment."

Application tips: The essential point of this exercise is to convey to participants the idea that the group is a safe space, where they can express themselves without fear or shame. The suggestions of rhythm, cadence, and authenticity of the "safe place" exercise also apply to this technique and most mental image techniques. If any participant finds the activity "silly" or "boring," encourage them to try or, alternatively, to imagine a more realistic object for them (such as a car or a cabin).

Feedback and Action Plan

Just like in the previous meeting, a closing discussion is held in which the therapists ask for feedback from the participants, encouraging them to share what they understood as the objectives of the session and what they learned. Those who feel comfortable can summarize the activities carried out. Everyone is encouraged to point out discomfort points so that the group can improve.

The therapists show the mode map to the participants, highlighting the blank space so that they can record their own interpretations of the modes. They can name and draw how they see each of these internal aspects. In addition, it is possible to give a group name for each mode, which will be recorded by the therapists for reference in future activities. The participants are guided to, in the action plan, draw their modes and circle the ones that make the most sense in their life stories. In this way, they can focus on perceiving them over the weeks and work on their regulation in the interventions.

The therapists remind the participants to bring their drawings, mode names, and reflections to share at the next meeting. In this session, they are asked to bring a childhood object that represents their child modes for the next meeting. It is not necessary to assign qualities to this object (such as good times or positive feelings); it is enough that it refers to childhood. If they do not have objects from this period, they can bring something that reminds them (e.g., a candy they ate when they were little).

Action plan: Deliver a summary about the modes to the participants; draw each mode and circle the ones that connect most with their life story.

Theme.

Understanding of basic concepts. Bring a significant childhood object.

Appendices and materials needed for Session 2
– Images that represent the schema modes, as mentioned in the program
– Basic description of the schema modes (appendix I) + action plan sheet

References

Cardoso, B. L. A., Paim, K., Catelan, R. F., & Liebross, E. H. (2022). Minority stress and the inner critic/oppressive sociocultural schema mode among sexual and gender minorities. *Current Psychology, 42*, 19991–19999. https://doi.org/10.1007/s12144-022-03086-y

Farrell, J. M., & Shaw, I. A. (2012). The course of group schema therapy stage one: Bonding and emotional regulation. In J. M. Farrell & I. A. Shaw (Eds.), *Group schema therapy for borderline personality disorder: A step-by-step treatment manual with patient workbook*. Wiley-Blackwell.

Farrell, J. M., & Shaw, I. A. (2018). *Experiencing schema therapy from the inside out: A self-practice/self-reflection workbook for therapists*. The Guilford Press.

Rafaeli, E., Bernstein, D. P., & Young, J. (2011). *Schema therapy*. Routledge

Trapp, R. (2024). "House" e "Lucifer": Deus e o diabo na terra da hipercompensação. In B. L. A. Cardoso & K. Paim (Eds.), *Terapia do esquema no cinema: os filmes e series na compreensão da prática clínica* (pp. 281–312). Artesã.

Wainer, R., & Rijo, D. (2016). O Modelo Teórico: Esquemas Iniciais Desadaptativos, Estilos de Enfrentamento e Modos Esquemáticos. In R. Wainer, K. Paim, R. Erdos, & R. Andriola (Eds.), *Terapia Cognitiva Focada em Esquemas: Integração em Psicoterapia* (pp. 47–67). Artmed.

Young, J. E., Klosko, J. S., & Weishaar, M. E. (2003). *Schema therapy: A practitioner's guide*. Guilford Press.

Further Reading

Cardoso, B. L. A., Lima, A. F. A., Costa, F. R. M., Loose, C., Liu, X., & Fabris, M. A. (2024). Sociocultural implications in the development of early maladaptive schemas in adolescents belonging to sexual and gender minorities. *International Journal of Environmental Research and Public Health, 21*(8). https://doi.org/10.3390/ijerph21080971

Farrell, J. M., & Shaw, I. A. (2020). Creative use of mode dialogues with the vulnerable child and dysfunctional critic modes. In J. S. Heath & M. Startup (Eds.), *Creative methods in schema therapy: Advances and innovation in clinical practice*. Routledge.

van der Wijngaart, R. (2021). *Imagery rescripting: Theory and practice*. Pavilion Publishing & Media.

Chapter 4
"How Society Influenced the Criticisms That I Internalized About Myself": Inner Critic Modes, Minority Stress, and Prejudice Against Sexual and Gender Diversity

The third session focuses on exploring, in a more in-depth way, the experiences and sufferings lived by sexual and gender minorities. During this session, therapists dedicate themselves to elucidating themes such as minority stress and stigma, providing participants with a broader understanding of how these factors can affect their mental health and influence their thoughts, emotions, and behaviors. The session also marks the beginning of the process of combating the inner critic (oppressive sociocultural) mode and strengthening the affirmative healthy adult mode—two themes that will be worked on more frequently throughout the intervention (Table 4.1).

Review of the Action Plan and Presentation of Childhood Objects

Without pressuring anyone to share more than they feel comfortable with, therapists validate the group's efforts and highlight the importance of the action plan for understanding individual emotional needs and behavior patterns. This moment also allows therapists to clarify the concept of schema modes, if necessary, and connect the previous activity with the current session, preparing the group for the new theme that will be addressed.

B. L. A. Cardoso, A. C. G. Braga, *The PRISMAS Group Therapy Handbook*,
https://doi.org/10.1007/978-3-031-91809-4_4

Table 4.1 Session activities and estimated duration

Activity/Intervention	Estimated duration
Review of the action plan and presentation of childhood objects	30 min
Understanding the inner critic modes through chairwork	40 min
Self-compassion exercise	20 min
Construction of coping cards	20 min
Feedback and action plan	10 min

Understanding Inner Critic Modes Through Chairwork

Objectives: To understand the inner critic modes, with an emphasis on the inner critic (oppressive sociocultural) mode; explore how judgments received throughout life (especially those related to sexual orientation and/or gender identity) may have impacted current self-image.

Procedure: This exercise is practical, aiming to psychoeducate the participants in an experiential way so that they feel more connected with the themes discussed, instead of passively absorbing them. To start it, therapists should organize three chairs at the front of the room, representing the three modes present in the intervention. They also need a balloon to symbolize the inner critic (oppressive sociocultural) mode and the object that represents each participant's child part. The activity has three stages.

The therapists explain the purpose and estimated duration of the exercise, about 40 min, highlighting that the goal is to explore the impact of the inner critic (oppressive sociocultural) mode on self-perception. It is important to stress that the activity takes place in a safe and welcoming environment. Three modes will be explored: the vulnerable child, the inner critic (oppressive sociocultural) mode, and the affirmative healthy adult. Two volunteers will be invited to take part, one for each rendition, as the activity will be performed twice. Therapists should explain that this experience can be emotionally challenging, but also transformative and positive. Those who feel comfortable can volunteer, without pressure to perform the activity in front of the group. The vulnerability of the volunteers should be valued, and the other participants are instructed to respond with respect and empathy.

One chair, on one side, will be designated for the vulnerable child, where the participant's representative object of childhood will be placed. Initially, the therapist assumes the role of the healthy adult, sitting in front of the child's chair (positioned so that the volunteer can also partially see him, behind the therapist, who plays the role of good protector). On the other side, the volunteer represents the inner critic (oppressive sociocultural) mode, holding a balloon or mask in front of their face or hands, visually indicating that they are in that mode without excessively identifying with it. The positions are illustrated in Fig. 4.1.

The volunteer who represents the inner critic (oppressive sociocultural) mode will be guided to express criticisms and judgments directed at the chair of the vulnerable child, especially those related to their sexual orientation and/or gender

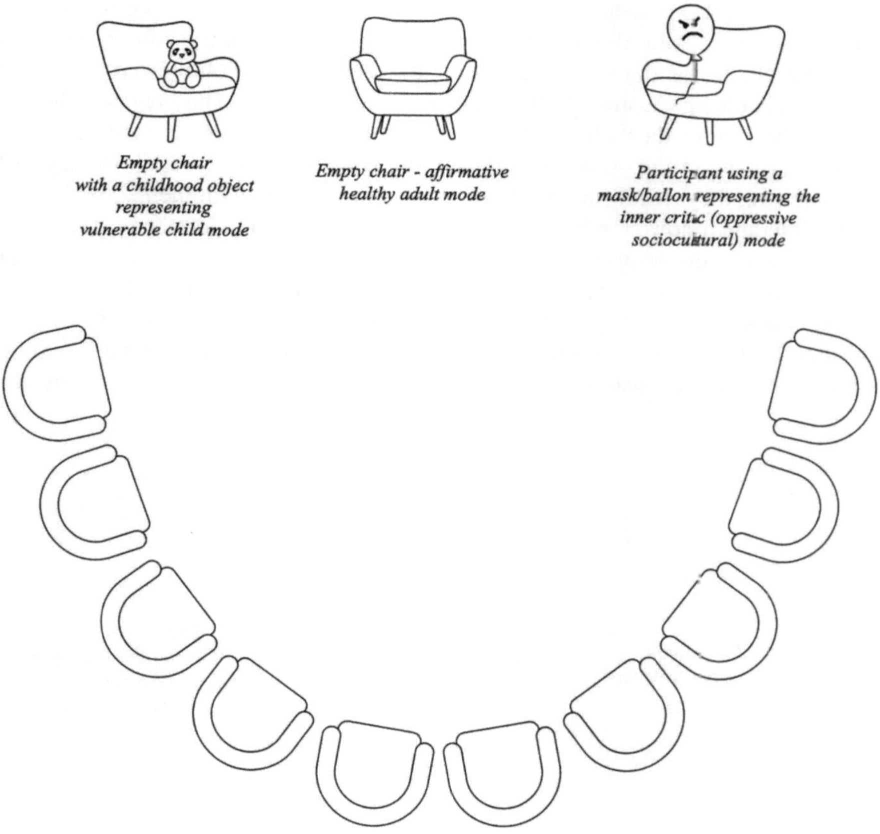

Fig. 4.1 Dialogue between the inner critic (oppressive sociocultural) mode and affirmative healthy adult mode

identity. They should bring up offenses, judgments, and retaliations that they usually direct at themselves or that they have heard from others at some point. The intention is that the exercise provides a cathartic effect, allowing them to express the critical voices that usually echo in their mind. The therapist, in the role of the healthy adult, will respond affirmatively, protecting the child with statements like: "'*Name of the participant's inner critic mode*', I will not allow you to speak like this with '*name of the participant's vulnerable child mode*'! They are just a child and do not deserve to hear this kind of thing"; or "What you are saying is harmful. It's homophobic (or transphobic, biphobic, etc. – the specific word chosen is at the therapist's discretion to match the client's context), and doesn't make any sense." This dialogue will continue until the participant feels that they have finished stating their criticisms that they have had to verbalize. Important: the first part should always end with the affirmative healthy adult having the last word, so as not to reinforce the inner critic (oppressive sociocultural) mode.

After the end of the first part, the volunteer is invited to leave the inner critic (oppressive sociocultural) mode chair and take the position of the vulnerable child, changing chairs for the second stage of the exercise and holding the childhood object. This change represents the transition to child mode. The previous chair is now symbolized by the balloon or mask of the inner critic (oppressive sociocultural) mode (as shown in Fig. 4.2). At this point, the volunteer can express how they feel when hearing the critical statements and how they resonate with them.

The therapist, now standing next to the participant, can guide them during this experience with questions like: "How was it to hear this from the '*name of the inner critic (oppressive sociocultural mode)*'?" "What do you feel you need now, '*name of the child mode*'?" "How was it to be protected from these statements?" It is essential that the therapist maintains an affirmative demeanor throughout the exercise, using correct terms (sexual orientation and not "sexual choice"), validating the

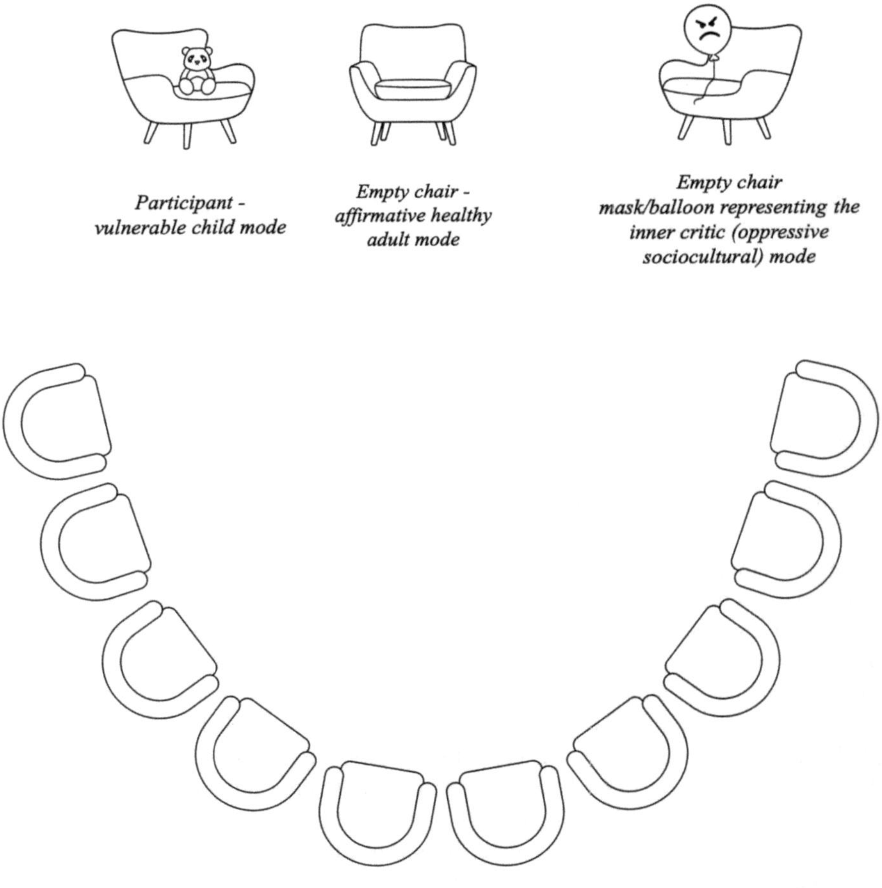

Fig. 4.2 Dialogue between Affirmative Healthy Adult and Vulnerable Child modes (therapist as the affirmative healthy adult mode)

participant's experiences ("there is nothing wrong with being who you are/loving who you love"), redirecting blame (reminding that society and prejudice against sexual and gender diversity are responsible for the feeling of inadequacy, not the person dealing with isolation), and offering comfort (providing a tissue, offering a hug, among other actions that make sense at the moment). If the relationship allows and the situation makes sense, the therapist can touch the participant's shoulder if the content is emotionally intense, demonstrating support and care. The therapist should be especially attentive to not commit microaggressions and, thus, avoid any iatrogenic behavior.

In the third phase, the volunteer participant is invited to take on the role of the affirmative healthy adult. The therapist, then, positions themselves next to the participant and observes, serving as an instructor if necessary—especially if the participant's healthy adult is not yet sufficiently strong and needs a caregiver model. In the role of the healthy adult, the volunteer, now sitting in the chair representing this mode, will address the childhood object, which remains in the chair of the vulnerable child, offering comfort and protection (as illustrated in Fig. 4.3). In this last part, the inner critic (oppressive sociocultural) mode is absent—the chair representing this mode is removed from the environment. If it is appropriate and genuine, the therapists can dramatize this removal, physically removing the chair from the room to symbolize that "it will not stand between us" and "will no longer participate in this conversation." The therapist can guide the participant with some questions and suggestions, such as: "What would you like to say to your child?"; "how could you take care of them now?"; "how and why is what the inner critic (oppressive sociocultural) mode said wrong? After all, they are just a child"; and "'*name of the participant's healthy adult mode*', what do you think this child needs to hear now to feel better?"

At the end of the intervention, the volunteer will be invited to return to their original chair and express how they felt during the experience, occupying those three modes in distinct phases—and how the interaction impacted them emotionally. They will be invited to pop the balloon of the inner critic (oppressive sociocultural) mode, in order to disempower it even more, symbolically. The other group members will be invited to share their perceptions about the exercise and to offer validation and affirmations to the volunteer, with each group member being able to say a sentence to encourage the participant volunteer's affirmative healthy adult.

Then, the second volunteer participant is invited to perform the activity, repeating the same process experienced previously by their group mate. The therapist will guide the discussion to ensure a supportive and empathetic environment. After the activity, the therapist will lead a reflection on the topics discussed during the experience, highlighting the importance of identifying and challenging the internalized voices modes, as well as the need for self-care and emotional support to confront them. They can also introduce the concept of minority stress, in a didactic and psychoeducational way—showing how the experience of prejudice against SGM can impact the formation of the inner critic (oppressive sociocultural) mode, in the face of an oppressive society.

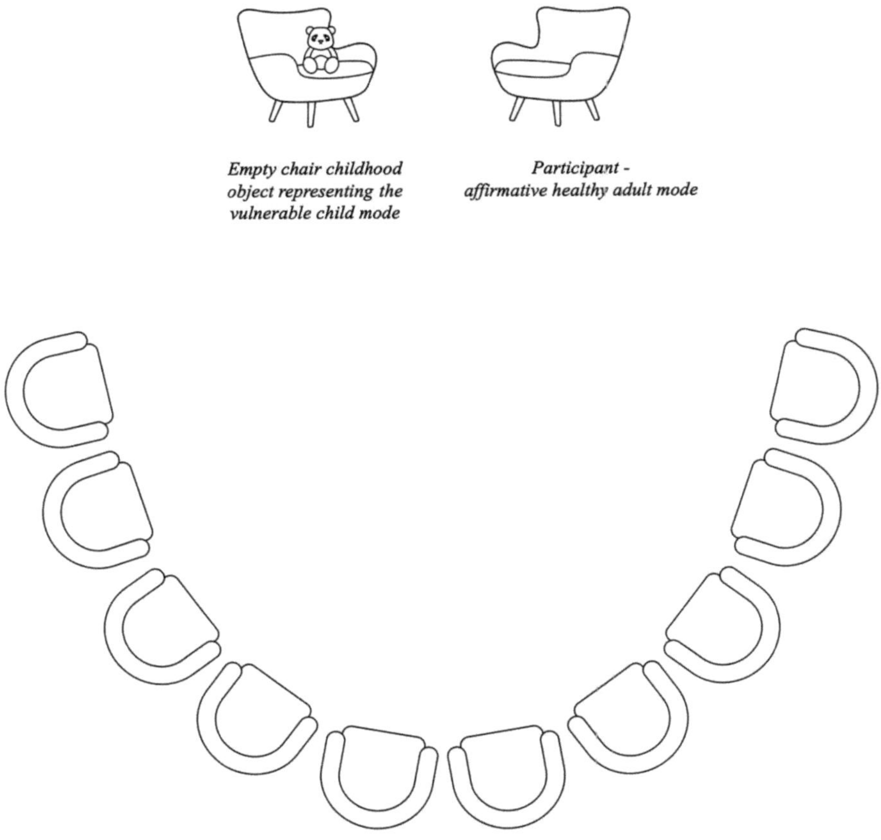

Fig. 4.3 Dialogue between Affirmative Healthy Adult and Vulnerable Child modes (participant as the affirmative healthy adult mode)

Minority stress: This concept, developed by Meyer (1995), refers to the combined tensions and stressors experienced by individuals who belong to marginalized minority groups. The focus given by therapists when explaining can be especially directed toward sexual orientation and/or gender identity, considering the theme of the group. People who belong to sexual and gender minorities may, for example, find themselves forced to hide an important part of their identity to protect their own physical well-being. Moreover, they internalize various negative views about themselves. They may feel excluded, inappropriate, or rejected. Also, the society around them can cause suffering, by preventing important access, such as to education or health. Visual elements (e.g., illustrations, figures, and cards) and the description of the inner critic (oppressive sociocultural) mode, present in Session 1, can be revisited to facilitate the chaining between sessions and the understanding of these dynamics in terms of ST by the participants. A more detailed and didactic description explaining some details of the inner critic (oppressive sociocultural) mode can be found in Appendix II.

Tips for application: it is necessary to be careful to, whenever the participant is in the chair, call them by the name they have selected for each of their modes and not by their real name. This is a necessary care so that the person does not feel directly confronted, but rather the inner critic (oppressive sociocultural) mode. The chairs used should also not, preferably, be the same ones used by the participants, so as not to create an unintentional stigma. These subtleties help to bring trust and security to the group.

Affirmative Practice: Compassion Technique

Objective: The therapists will guide the participants in a compassionate practice with the aim of developing an affirmative and self-accepting attitude. This practice aims to cultivate the ability of empathy and kindness both toward oneself and toward others (based on Consenza, 2021).

Procedure: The practice occurs in stages of connection with different people: first with a loved one, then with oneself, and finally with the other members of the group. After this sequence, which aims to develop both compassion and self-compassion, the therapist encourages participants to direct pleasant thoughts and feelings to colleagues, promoting a positive connection within the group. At the end of the exercise, the therapists reserve a moment to reflect on the group experience. It is essential that the therapist narrates the exercise slowly, ideally participating in the practice along with the group. Doing the exercise in a hurry can cause agitation and feelings of anxiety or distress in the participants. Therefore, it is important to control the voice, speak slowly, and allow for a few seconds between each sentence, thus promoting a calm and welcoming environment.

Narration of the activity: "To start our next activity, I ask that you close your eyes and take a few deep breaths. Before we start, find a comfortable position that allows you to be present in an attentive and relaxed way. (Pause). Let's dedicate a few moments to breathe consciously, counting the cycles of breathing or simply feeling the flow of air in the body.

Now, I invite you to imagine a loved one, someone with whom you have a good friendship. (Pause). Bring to your mind images of moments when this person may have faced difficulties, misunderstandings, fatigue, anxiety, and insecurity. Also think about their dreams, desires, and their achievements and joys. (Pause). Realize that, just like you, this person seeks to have a good life and be free from suffering. If it makes sense to you, try to direct to this person phrases of compassion. (Pause). For example, you may wish that they are calm, free from suffering, and safe. Or, if you prefer, simply imagine sending pleasant emotions to them. (Pause).

Now, let's slowly change our mental picture. I ask that you now imagine yourself. (Pause). Remember, with affection, moments when you went through difficulties, misunderstandings, fatigue, anxiety, and insecurity. What do you dream of? What are your desires? What happy moments, achievements, and joys have you lived? (Pause). Realize that, just like the loved one, you also seek to have a good life and be free from suffering. (Pause). Now, try to direct to yourself phrases of compassion. For example, you may wish to be calm, free from suffering, and safe. Or, if you prefer, just imagine sending pleasant emotions internally. (Pause).

For the next step of this practice, I ask that you open your eyes when I ring the bell (or, if you don't have a bell, just "When I let you know"), but still remain silent and in a contemplative mindset. '*Bell ring*'. Open your eyes and observe the people present in this room. (Pause). Try to take them in well, noting in your mind their physical characteristics and what is striking about them. Now, when I ring the bell again, I ask that you close your eyes. '*Bell ring*'. Close your eyes and imagine what the people around you may be going through, what challenges or difficulties they may be facing. (Pause). If it's difficult to visualize everyone at the same time, bring just one person to your mind. Direct empathy and understanding to this person. (Pause). Also try to think about the dreams, desires, and joys that they may have. (Pause). Once again, if it's easier for you, think of just one person at a time. '*Bell ring*'. Open your eyes and try to direct joy and compassion to the other participants. Try to connect with each person's emotions, observing their expressions and looking each person in the eyes. (Pause). Close your eyes and spend a few moments in contact with what this experience made you feel. (Pause). Gradually, release the mental images, keeping the sensations of compassion and goodwill. Return your attention to your breath, inhaling and exhaling deeply a few times. (Pause). When you feel ready, open your eyes, ending the experience."

Tips for application: In addition to what has already been described in the other imagery techniques, an important suggestion here is to succinctly explain the concepts of compassion and self-compassion to the participants before starting the practice. It is also interesting to ask them in advance to think of a loved one, without explaining the reason. This way, confusion in choosing someone during the practice is avoided and the exercise is not biased.

Building Coping Cards

Objectives: To provide a first healthy strategy to cope with internalized self-criticism.

Procedure: Therapists can start the discussion by asking in an exploratory and curious way: "You saw the experience of your colleague in the chair exercise and now had the opportunity to get in touch with your own healthy side. Our next activity seeks to solidify what we have experienced here. What would you say to your own inner critic, countering it, if you had the chance? What did you say to the loved one when you sent them compassion and what could you say to yourselves? If your best friend said the same negative things about themselves that you say to yourself, how would you respond?" Then, the therapists allow the participants to respond, helping them to form new healthy thoughts that can counter internal criticisms. They can explain that one of the simplest ways to deal with criticisms and oppressions is to bring alternative ideas to one's own mind. The consistency in repeating a healthy, positive attitude about something to oneself is capable of generating changes in the way one sees a situation. A suggestion of how to explain this is: "Let's think that you work from home, sitting all day. Maybe some of you are used to home office and have this experience. Well, after a year of working this way, you go to the doctor and find out that your spine is partially crooked because of a bad office chair. He explains that, to improve this, you need not only a new chair, but also to break the old habit that the bad chair created - this means actively sitting in the right way and adjusting your back during the day. The first step to this is to realize that you are sitting crookedly. The second is to adjust your back in the new chair. The third is to repeat this countless times - it's not magic. You took a year to have effects of the bad chair on your spine and now you will need some time to return it to a healthy position. Notice, the new ergonomic chair is essential! But just buying it and continuing to sit wrong in it is not enough. It's the same idea with the coping cards: it's not enough to know the healthy thought; we have to bring it to mind whenever we notice that it has escaped to the criticisms and repeat whenever necessary, until our brain fully adopts the new information. The good side is that, just like adjusting the spine, changing your way of thinking will decrease the pain, wear and tear, and discomfort, which perhaps you didn't even realize were there until you tried the comfortable chair."

Thus, each participant will be instructed to compile a list addressing how the inner critic (oppressive sociocultural) mode and, consequently, minority stress affect their thoughts, emotions, and behaviors. The focus is on identifying patterns and seeing them as a part of a self that has been hurt, but not as a truth about who they are. In this way, they will be able to disassociate themselves from excessive self-criticism.

Part of the task includes listing alternative thoughts and positive affirmations that they can make to themselves when the criticisms arise more strongly. The idea is to assemble coping cards from what was listed, disempowering the inner critic modes daily. The therapists will be able to present a reference (Table 4.2) or print it and deliver these forms to the participants. It should be noted that this is an exercise that will continue to be valid and important even after the end of the 12 sessions. Similarly, it is not a magic solution in itself; it is just a start of change. They can

Table 4.2 Model of coping card for thoughts linked to the inner critic (oppressive sociocultural) mode, through affirmative thoughts

Thoughts linked to the inner critic (oppressive sociocultural) mode that I frequently have	Affirmative and healthy thoughts to counter it
Example: "*I am strange and will never be able to be loved for being LGBTQIA+* "	Example: "*Even though I still can't feel totally good about who I am, I know that eventually I will be able to look at myself with affection. I can see other LGBTQIA+ people and perceive them as happy and deserving of love. Why wouldn't I be?*"
Example: "*My existence is a sin and god will punish me*"	Example: "*There are several religions and, even within the Christianity, several ways of seeing the same bible. I can believe in a fair and understanding god, who loves me as I am*"

conclude: "Just as to improve our spine we will need not only to adjust the posture, but also weight training, physical therapy, and massages, the coping cards are one of several resources that we will learn to use together. Perhaps they are more useful for some people, while for others they seem less effective. Fortunately, we will still assemble together a very complete and interesting toolbox, throughout our process."

Feedback and Action Plan

For the next session, participants are advised to continue assembling their coping cards, based on the thoughts they identify throughout the week. Ideally, they should notice the presence of the inner critic (oppressive sociocultural) mode and record the cognitions that arise in this context. They should also continue listing alternative and healthier ways of thinking. The idea is that they try to reread the cards several times a day—whenever they notice themselves falling into self-criticism or simply remember the existence of the cards. Participants are encouraged to bring their reflections and insights to share at the next meeting, and therapists are available to support and clarify any doubts that may arise during the action plan.

Action Plan: Continue assembling the coping cards and rereading them during the week.

Appendices and materials needed for Session 3
– A bell or other object that can be used to mark the beginning and end of meditation practice
– Description of the inner critic (oppressive sociocultural) mode (Appendix II)
– Sheets of paper or cards to create the "coping cards" (available in Appendix III)

References

Consenza, R. M. (2021). *Neurociência e Mindfulness: meditação, equilíbrio emocional e redução do estresse*. Artmed.

Meyer, I. H. (1995). Minority stress and mental health in gay men. *Journal of Health and Social Behavior, 36*(1), 38–56. https://doi.org/10.2307/2137286

Further Reading

Cardoso, B. L. A., Lima, A. F. A., Costa, F. R. M., Loose, C., Liu, X., & Fabris, M. A. (2024). Sociocultural implications in the development of early maladaptive schemas in adolescents belonging to sexual and gender minorities. *International Journal of Environmental Research and Public Health, 21*(8). https://doi.org/10.3390/ijerph21080971

Cardoso, B. L. A., Paim, K., Catelan, R. F., & Liebross, E. H. (2022). Minority stress and the inner critic/oppressive sociocultural schema mode among sexual and gender minorities. *Current Psychology, 42*, 19991–19999. https://doi.org/10.1007/s12144-022-03086-y

Farrell, J. M., & Shaw, I. A. (2020). Creative use of mode dialogues with the vulnerable child and dysfunctional critic modes. In J. S. Heath & M. Startup (Eds.), *Creative methods in schema therapy: Advances and innovation in clinical practice*. Routledge.

Farrell, J. M., & Shaw, I. A. (2018). *Experiencing schema therapy from the inside out: A self-practice/self-reflection workbook for therapists*. The Guilford Press.

Farrell, J. M., & Shaw, I. A. (2012). *Group schema therapy for borderline personality disorder: A step-by-step treatment manual with patient workbook*. Wiley-Blackwell.

Meyer, I. H. (2003). Prejudice, social stress, and mental health in lesbian, gay, and bisexual populations: Conceptual issues and research evidence. *Psychological Bulletin, 129*(5), 674–697. https://doi.org/10.1037/0033-2909.129.5.674

Young, J. E., Klosko, J. S., & Weishaar, M. E. (2003). *Schema therapy: A practitioner's guide*. Guilford Press.

Chapter 5
"Knowing and Highlighting My Strengths": Strengthening the Affirmative Healthy Adult Mode

The fourth meeting aims to explore the discovery and strengthening of the affirmative healthy adult in a more in-depth and practical way. Through dynamics, thematic experiences, and a guided discovery approach, therapists guide participants to identify which stimuli elicit the emergence of their affirmative healthy adult. During this session, group members have the opportunity to recognize their own personal strengths, as well as identify areas that still need to be developed. All of this is conducted in a welcoming and positive manner, with the intention of celebrating sexual diversity, in contrast to the cisheteronormative culture, which often silences and oppresses (Table 5.1).

Action Plan Review

Participants are invited to share, if they feel comfortable, the thoughts they noted down last week. Therapists can remind them of what the inner critic (oppressive sociocultural) mode is and how it impacts the well-being of sexual and gender minorities (SGM). From the examples brought, the group is encouraged to explore how these cognitions resonated individually, highlighting the destructive power of this mode.

Table 5.1 Session activities and estimated duration

Activity/Intervention	Estimated duration
Action plan review	15 min
Identifying your healthy adult	30 min
Identifying pots of modes and the role of the healthy adult	35 min
Finding the healthy adult within me	30 min
Feedback and action plan	10 min

B. L. A. Cardoso, A. C. G. Braga, *The PRISMAS Group Therapy Handbook*,
https://doi.org/10.1007/978-3-031-91809-4_5

Finally, alternative thoughts can also be presented, with the group expanding the discussion and proposing new possibilities to disempower these oppressive thoughts. Therapists can question about action strategies or ways to deal with emotions that could contribute even more to this disempowerment. In addition, they can ask if participants noticed any emotional or cognitive difference by keeping the coping cards close, as well as the frequency of use. They always should highlight that long-term results require extensive repetition of these activities.

The transition to the current session can be made by explaining that, while criticisms and oppressions must be combated, the healthy side needs to be stimulated and strengthened for an effective change to occur. These modes are in a kind of balance: the more the healthy adult mode gains strength, the weaker the inner critic (oppressive sociocultural) mode becomes. With this in mind, the following activities aim at strengthening personal potentialities, expanding the care repertoire beyond combating the negative side.

Identifying Your Healthy Adult

Objectives: To identify positive and strengthened characteristics that make up one's own healthy adult; transform negative thoughts about oneself.

Procedure: In this intervention, therapists present the concept of the "healthy adult"and its importance in self-perception and personal development. In an interactive and dialogic manner, participants are invited to identify characteristics of their own healthy adult. An affirmative attitude is encouraged during the practice to promote the development of this view in the group.

Therapists can propose questions to facilitate reflection, such as:

1. What songs make you feel good, and why? How can they be linked to the characteristics you possess or would like to develop?
2. How do you act when you feel confident and secure? What behaviors do you value in yourself at these times?
3. Is there a phrase or quote that inspires you and reinforces a positive feeling? It can be a personal mantra or a quote from a movie or series.
4. What are the strengths you recognize in yourself? Is there a recent challenge that you managed to face well?
5. What flaws do you notice in other people that you notice that you do not have? If it's hard to identify qualities in yourself, a good way might be to think about what you don't have that's negative.
6. Do you have any interesting skills, even if it's something simple?
7. If you were to quantify, from 0 to 100, what percentage of your actions today are guided by the healthy adult?
8. How do you access your "healthy adult"? In what situations does it manifest most strongly?
9. How would your future be different if you had constant access to the healthy adult?

10. At what moments did you notice your affirmative side of the healthy adult? In which situations did you feel comfortable or even proud of your sexuality and/or gender identity?

After a time for individual reflection, participants are invited to share their answers, if they feel comfortable. Therapists should highlight that there are no right or wrong answers. The healthy adult is unique, flexible, and creative. The activity ends with a discussion on how these positive characteristics can be cultivated and used in everyday situations, especially in times of challenge or stress. Therapists emphasize that the healthy adult mode is essential for us to be dedicated, productive, and caring, as well as practicing self-care. It represents our wisest and most refined version.

This practical intervention not only provides psychoeducation but also encourages change, by stimulating participants to recognize and value their strengths and internal resources. It promotes a deep connection among group members and enables the learning of strategies to nurture positive qualities. In addition, by hearing examples from peers, they can be inspired to further develop characteristics of their own healthy version.

Some participants, especially those with self-esteem difficulties or who are beginning their contact with their own sexual orientation and/or gender identity, may have difficulty identifying and describing qualities. In this case, a suggestion is to ask participants to ask family and/or friends to point out positive characteristics. Another possibility is for the group members themselves to indicate a quality of each colleague, although it is important for therapists to assess the suitability of this approach to avoid causing discomfort or embarrassment.

Another relevant piece of information to be communicated is that the healthy adult also has flaws and moments of vulnerability; he does not need to be perfect or always right. The proposal is to value their positive qualities and connect to the process of self-discovery, learning, and continuously improving. A good healthy adult believes in himself, trusts his potential, and is open to constructive feedback.

Next, therapists can present some specific characteristics of the healthy adult mode, reminding participants that all human beings possess this mode to some degree. What varies is the level of strength and the frequency of activation of this mode. No one is 0% or 100% healthy adult, and we are always in a continuous process of developing this dimension of ourselves.

It is important to note that, in the case of LGBTQIA+ people, one of the facets of the healthy adult is the affirmative side. This aspect manifests especially when the individual feels proud of their identity and expresses their sexuality in an empowered way. For this, it is necessary to be even stronger, kinder, and more compassionate with oneself, as these people face a society that often minimizes them and tries to restrict their shine and strength through offensive comments and/or erasing their gender identity or sexual orientation (Cardoso et al., 2022).

For this reason, when working with SGM, who already tend to have a more negative self-image, it is crucial to adopt a positive and validating attitude toward peers and oneself. In addition to explaining these concepts, therapists should demonstrate this position in their attitudes, adopting an affirmative and welcoming behavior. They should also mediate interactions between participants so that everyone adopts this same care, internalizing an adult model that incorporates LGBTQIA+ pride.

Below are gathered some of the central characteristics of the healthy adult mode, which will serve as a guide for therapists and participants (based on Farrell & Shaw, 2012). It is worth noting that all people exercise these aspects throughout life, continuously. It is not necessary for someone to already master all these points; the goal is to see them as a guide and an inspiration for long-term development.

1. Being aware of your beliefs, needs, values, and internal feelings.
2. Feeling that you regulate your own feelings and needs, instead of being impulsively controlled by them.
3. Being able to maintain your values, beliefs, feelings, and needs even in the face of people who activate your emotions (such as authority figures or those who provoke insecurity).
4. Clearly expressing your feelings, beliefs, and internal needs, without feeling guilty or minimizing what you feel.
5. Maintaining a constant sense of "Self" in all situations and circumstances, without confusion about what you really feel or want, having clarity and pride in who you are.
6. Seeking meaningful personal values, living according to your worldview.
7. Maintaining an internal sense of "centering," especially in times of stress, being able to organize your thoughts in situations that require it (such as in family crises or at work).
8. Establish clear boundaries between yourself and others, being able to connect and, at the same time, maintain autonomy.
9. Maintain self-esteem and a positive and coherent view of oneself, without depending on the validation of others.
10. Adopt an assertive stance on important issues, knowing how to position yourself.
11. Trust in your intuition and feelings, without doubting yourself and your perceptions.
12. Take pride in who you are, achieving comfort and validation in relation to your sexuality and identity.

Identifying Pots of Modes and the Role of the Healthy Adult

Objectives: To raise awareness about the function of each mode and its coexistence with others; strengthen the affirmative healthy adult as a leader; disempower/combat the inner critic (oppressive sociocultural) mode. Identify automatic thoughts and associate them with different modes.

Procedure: The therapists start by explaining that everyone has, internally, several different parts. For this session, these parts will be visually represented with pots. The therapists arrange eleven pots on a central surface, each representing a mode, using the images and/or names given in the first session to maintain participants' familiarity with the content. The therapists can use a metaphor to illustrate the arrangement of the pots and how the dynamics between them work.

The child modes are presented as intense and sincere, clearly expressing their feelings and primary needs, and are placed at the back of the table. At this moment, the participants are invited to say moments in their lives when they perceived themselves guided by strong and primary emotions and what they wanted to communicate in relation to their emotional needs.

Then, the coping modes are presented and placed in front of the children, to illustrate an attempt at protection (e.g., disconnecting from the situation, overdoing it with drinking, accepting an uncomfortable situation). Participants are encouraged to share examples of situations in which these sides appeared and/or were useful in their lives.

The healthy adult is positioned as a leader in front of everyone, symbolizing its balancing role. Opposite the healthy adult is the inner critic (oppressive sociocultural) mode, which tries to lead in a destructive way. The therapists explain that, during the group, the participants are learning to give more space to the affirmative healthy adult, promoting balance and harmony among the modes.

For this activity, each participant is instructed to list five thoughts they had throughout the week. Then, the therapists collect the group's papers, folded randomly (so as not to expose anyone), and open them one by one, asking the participants to classify in which pot that thought should go, according to the characteristics of each mode. The therapists can start the exercise by providing some personal (or hypothetical) examples to show the typical way each mode thinks (they can consult Session 1 again, in case of doubts to prepare this presentation). Figure 5.1 also presents a model of the pots that can be assembled for the intervention (the images to print and cut out, of each character, are found in the Appendices).

Experience: Finding the Healthy Adult Within Me

Objectives: To promote psychoeducation; help participants to understand their own emotional reactions; encourage self-assertion; strengthen identity and self-efficacy.

Procedure: In this intervention, the therapists invite the participants to reflect on a moment when they felt empowered and capable of affirming their own identity. Through a visualization exercise, participants are guided to mentally relive that moment, focusing on the physical sensations and emotions it arouses. This process allows them to connect more deeply with the thoughts, sensations, and emotions associated with their healthy adult, facilitating the recognition of this mode in future situations.

Narration of the activity: "For our next activity, we will try to get in touch with our healthy adult. Find a comfortable position, close your eyes, take a deep breath, and relax." (Pause). Let's revisit a special memory, a moment when you felt strong and capable of asserting your own identity. It can be a memory from the past or

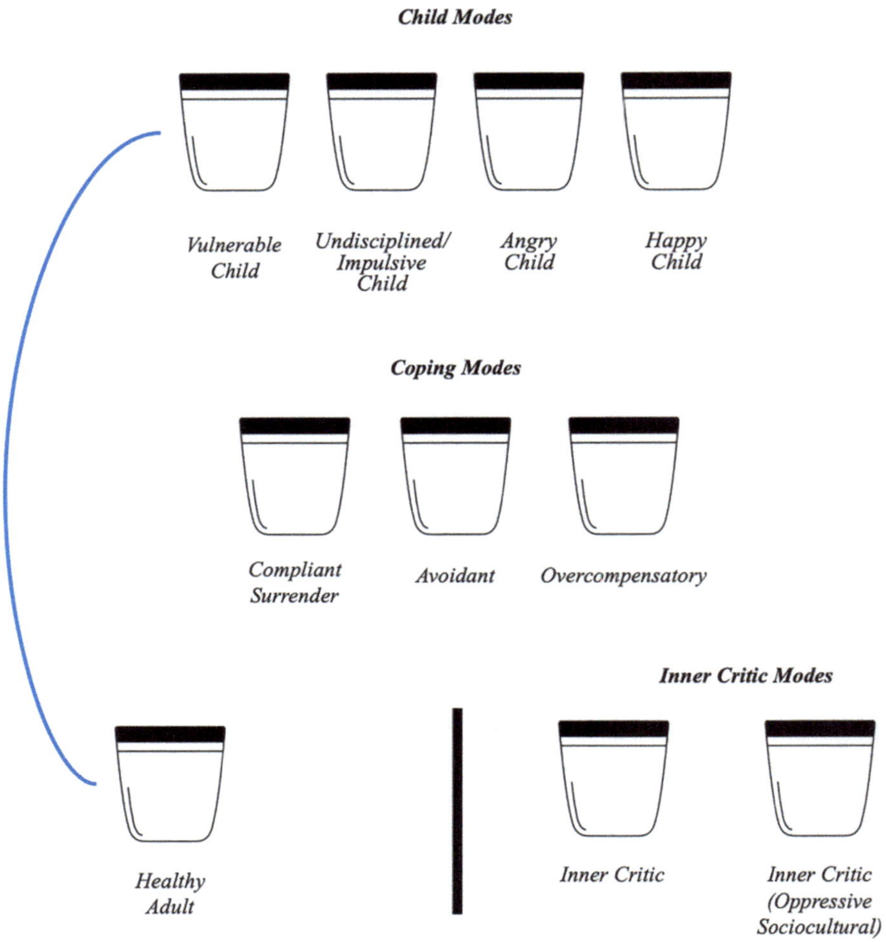

Fig. 5.1 Pots of modes, arranged in rows of modes, according to psychoeducation

something more recent. If it's difficult to bring something to mind, you can imagine what it would be like to assert yourself and live fully as you are, genuinely, in the future." (Pause).

Allow yourself to immerse in this memory or mental image. Remember the details: colors, sounds, smells, textures. (Pause). Feel the emotions of that moment. What were you doing? Was there anyone with you? Was there anything that stuck with you? Did you feel any physical sensation? What feelings arose?

This is your moment. A moment when you were strong, assertive, and true to who you are. (Pause). Celebrate this experience and feel the strength that comes from being authentically yourself. Let's spend some time here, in silence, just reliving this experience. You can add new details or dialogues that intensify this feeling of self-confidence and belonging. (Pause). We are celebrating you, in your own way.

And, after a while, I invite you to share your experiences, if you wish, so that we can celebrate these affirming moments together. Remember, there is no rush. This is your moment, your memory, your feeling. Allow yourself to fully immerse in this experience. (Pause). If any volunteer feels ready, I ask them to start narrating their mental image, still with their eyes closed (therapist calls on the participant and asks them to briefly describe the scene). Let's all visualize the scene narrated by your colleague, keeping our eyes closed. (Pause). Imagine how they might be feeling. Now, in a clockwise direction, I will ask everyone to share a bit of their scene, so we can imagine together. If this is uncomfortable for you, feel free to just say how you feel when imagining this version of yourself. As each one narrates their story, we will all imagine it and celebrate our colleague. (Each participant narrates their scene, being guided by the therapist.)

So, when you are ready, take a deep breath once again and slowly allow these images to fade away. Return to your breathing, to the here and now. (Pause). Move slowly some parts of the body and, when you feel ready, you can open your eyes. And remember, you can always return to this memory when you need to strengthen yourselves."

Feedback and Action Plan

At the end of the meeting, the therapists again request feedback from participants, maintaining an attitude of acceptance and openness. They try to summarize what was discussed, highlighting the main points, and seek to understand what was most significant or impactful for the participants.

For the action plan, the therapists explain that, based on the discussions of the meeting, each participant can identify and define which behaviors are most characteristic of their healthy adult mode. As guidance, they can consider some questions, like:

- Which behaviors or attitudes do I feel strengthen my identity?
- What actions help me maintain calm and centered in challenging moments?
- How do I usually communicate when I am in my healthy adult side?
- In what way do I demonstrate self-acceptance and compassion for myself?
- In what situations have I been proud of who I am?

These suggestions for reflective questions will be passed on to the participants by the instructors. In addition to thinking or listing these behaviors, it is suggested that they try to be more connected to their affirmative healthy adult in the next week, repeating these behaviors actively. Even if it seems silly or difficult, it is interesting to proceed, to change little by little. The process of behavioral change, through repetition and habit creation, can be briefly explained to motivate the participants.

The therapists share these suggestions for reflective questions with the participants. In addition to just thinking or listing these behaviors, participants are encouraged to try to connect more with their affirmative healthy adult in the next week, repeating these behaviors intentionally and actively.

Even if the exercise may seem silly or challenging, it is important to continue, as small changes, when made consistently, can have a big impact over time. The therapists can briefly explain that the process of behavioral change strengthens through repetition and habit creation, helping to consolidate this new way of acting and thinking. By seeing these actions as steps toward personally growing stronger, participants may feel more motivated to incorporate them into their daily lives.

Action plan: "Developing the healthy adult" exercise, as previously described.

Appendices and materials needed for Session 4
– Small boxes to carry out the pot's activity
– Images of characters printed or drawn according to appendix I descriptions
– Sheets with the characteristics of the healthy adult, according to Appendix IV

References

Cardoso, B. L. A., Paim, K., Catelan, R. F., & Liebross, E. H. (2022). Minority stress and the inner critic/oppressive sociocultural schema mode among sexual and gender minorities. *Current Psychology, 42*, 19991–19999. https://doi.org/10.1007/s12144-022-03086-y

Farrell, J. M., & Shaw, I. A. (2012). *Group schema therapy for borderline personality disorder: A step-by-step treatment manual with patient workbook*. Wiley-Blackwell.

Further Reading

Cardoso, B. L. A., Lima, A. F. A., Costa, F. R. M., Loose, C., Liu, X., & Fabris, M. A. (2024). Sociocultural implications in the development of early maladaptive schemas in adolescents belonging to sexual and gender minorities. *International Journal of Environmental Research and Public Health, 21*(8). https://doi.org/10.3390/ijerph21080971

Farrell, J. M., & Shaw, I. A. (2020). Creative use of mode dialogues with the vulnerable child and dysfunctional critic modes. In J. S. Heath & M. Startup (Eds.), *Creative methods in schema therapy: Advances and innovation in clinical practice*. Routledge.

Rafaeli, E., Bernstein, D. P., & Young, J. (2011). *Schema therapy*. Routledge.

van der Wijngaart, R. (2021). *Imagery rescripting: Theory and practice*. Pavilion Publishing & Media.

Young, J. E., Klosko, J. S., & Weishaar, M. E. (2003). *Schema therapy: A practitioner's guide*. Guilford Press.

Chapter 6
"Connecting with My History": Deepening Self-knowledge About How What I Went Through Influenced Who I Am

Session 5 aims to consolidate the learnings acquired so far, serving as a closure of the introductory part of the intervention. With this in mind, the session deepens the participants' knowledge about the healthy adult mode and provides self-care tools that can be derived from this mode. This aims to prepare the participants for more intense interventions that will occur in the second part of the program. In addition, this session initiates an activity of coping and disempowering the inner critic (oppressive sociocultural) mode, connecting directly with the next steps of the intervention (Table 6.1).

Review of the Action Plan

Therapists can start the session by asking participants which of them feel comfortable sharing with the group a little about their own affirmative healthy adult. They recall the aspects used to find it (ways of speaking, thinking, relating, problem-solving, acting, etc.) and ask for examples of situations, cognitions, and behaviors that represent this mode. They can also ask which points are already strong in this mode and what still needs to be strengthened.

The second part of the action plan involved trying to access this mode more frequently during the week, from the stimuli that activate it. Therapists can ask how this experience was and if performing this task represented a challenge for the participants. They can help them list elements that connect them with their healthy adult (i.e., songs, smells, striking phrases, TV shows) and even identify common aspects among the healthy adults of all the participants. In this way, it is possible to create a list of strategies to activate this mode during the session, which also contributes to strengthen the relationship between the participants and the sense of belonging to the group.

B. L. A. Cardoso, A. C. G. Braga, *The PRISMAS Group Therapy Handbook*,
https://doi.org/10.1007/978-3-031-91809-4_6

Table 6.1 Session activities and estimated duration

Activity/Intervention	Estimated duration
Review of the action plan	15 min
Imagery exercise: The healthy adult	20 min
Letter to the inner critic (oppressive sociocultural) mode	30 min
Conversation about the five core emotional needs	25 min
Good parents exercise, reduced version	20 min
Feedback and action plan	10 min

As the group is composed of SGM, it is crucial to always adopt an affirmative stance. Therapists should help participants identify their positive qualities, remind them of the courage it takes to showcase themselves and speak in public, and highlight the strengths and personal pride of each one. Individuals belonging to SGM usually have a history of attacks on self-esteem. Reversing this situation with a careful and welcoming approach is essential. In addition, this stance serves as a model for the participants, who can replicate this process of affirmation with their colleagues and themselves.

The current session integrates the assumptions of the two previous meetings, demonstrating in a practical way how the strengthened affirmative healthy adult can be used to deal effectively and functionally with the inner critic (oppressive sociocultural) mode. Activities focused on these two modes alternate, allowing the consolidation of understanding about their functioning, as they will be key pieces in the rest of the intervention. The therapists can explain this to the participants, in addition to introducing that, from the next meeting, the focus will be on more practical ways of seeking changes, considering that the bases of the therapeutic process are already solidified for everyone.

Imagery Exercise: The Healthy Adult

Objectives: To solidify contact with the healthy adult; visualize their own healthy adult through imagery exercise.

After reviewing the action plan, therapists ask the participants to close their eyes and take some deep breaths. Then, they start the narration.

Narration of the activity: "I ask you to bring to mind the image of you, the way you are today. Imagine that you are safe and sitting alone in our room. Try to focus on each aspect that defines you. (Pause). Notice every detail of your appearance, of your being. Note what makes you who you are. (Pause). Now, your best version will enter the room. It is not a perfect version, an unreachable figure, but rather simply represents your side that includes your best traits. All your qualities shine and stand out in this way of being. What is this side like? Observe it for some time. (Pause). This version also includes the points that you have been trying to develop, the things you aspire to be in the short and medium term. What are the habits and routine of this part of you? How does it dress, how does it act with those around you? Try to contemplate this. (Pause). There may be a desire for comparison or self-criticism, but remember: this healthy side already exists within you. It is an important part, which you are working on here, in our group, so that it appears more and more. This version is welcoming and kind. (Pause) Try to imagine your healthy adult taking care of you, directing words and actions that make you feel good and emotionally nourished at this moment. (Pause). Experience what it is like to be cared for by yourself. (Pause).

Now, imagine this side returning inside you. Even though you are alone in the room again, the healthy adult accompanies you wherever you go. They are an essential and necessary part of you (Pause). Now, slowly, each of us will enter the room, bringing with us our healthy adult. I will start. I will sit in the chair where I always sit, facing you. Now the 'co-therapist's name' will enter. Shall we say 'hi' and wave to them? I will say the name of each one of us now, clockwise. When I say yours, you don't need to open your eyes - you are already in your own imagined space. Shall we enter the room then? (The therapist continues, narrating the name of each participant). Now, let this image go, returning to the present moment and to our real room. I ask you to breathe deeply five more times. (Pause). Make small movements in your body, in your arms and legs. Move your neck. (Pause). When you are ready, open your eyes, ending the exercise."

Application tips: Therapists can take advantage of the fact that the previous exercise connects with the current one to ask participants how it was to perceive their own healthy adult through imagery exercise. An interesting question would be: "How can you do to achieve even more your best version? What qualities of yours already stand out?" This reflection allows group members to explore personal aspects that need to be strengthened while further affirming the healthy sides of their personality.

Letter to the Inner Critic (Oppressive Sociocultural) Mode

Objectives: To combat/disempower the inner critic (oppressive sociocultural) mode; allow a new view of painful situations from personal history; assign new meaning to experiences.

Procedure: This exercise can be the most emotionally activating of the session, making it essential that therapists conduct it with a welcoming and careful demeanor. After the previous interventions, which aim to strengthen the healthy facets of the participants, they are invited to write a letter to the symbolic figure that represents the inner critic (oppressive sociocultural) mode. The focus is to take advantage of the motivation generated by the previous exercises to confront this mode directly. In the letter, participants should think of something that symbolizes this mode. It can be a person who was very critical in the past, a character, society as a whole, or even a completely new figure, to which they will give a name. The important thing is that this figure represents, in some way, anti-LGBT comments or the prejudiced context to which they were exposed, and that has contributed to the internalization of oppressive messages.

Participants are encouraged to express their feelings and thoughts, opposing the speeches of the inner critic (sociocultural oppressor) mode with an alternative and affirmative view. The letter should function as a direct dialogue with this mode, allowing emotional expression. To facilitate this connection, it is suggested that patients close their eyes and remember situations in which they felt invalidated or criticized because of their sexual orientation and/or gender identity. If they cannot remember something specific, they can reflect on moments when they felt prevented from being who they really are or attacked for it. After this brief reflection, they should open their eyes and start free writing, pouring onto paper the emotions that arise. They can, for example, describe how these criticisms impacted their lives, expose grievances related to these experiences, and explore other emotions linked to the theme. During the process, it is essential that the therapists offer support to any participant who shows discomfort or disturbance. The co-therapist, in particular, should be attentive to provide directed care, if necessary. The writing aims directly to decrease the influence of the inner critic (oppressive sociocultural) mode on the participants. Therefore, it is important to instruct them to directly oppose the harsh words they heard about themselves.

The therapists explain that the participants will have about 10–15 min to write, in a calm and private manner. It is essential to highlight that no one should invade the space or look at another group member's letter. The exercise is deeply personal, and the sincere connection with the activity is crucial to promote changes.

The activity helps participants to directly confront the inner critic (oppressive sociocultural) mode as if it were a real character in their lives, promoting a dialogue in the first person. The letter should be explicitly addressed to this figure, person or institution, so that the experience is more real and emotionally linked. Thinking in a distant or third-party way can disconnect the participants from their emotions, while confronting something more concrete intensifies the experience.

In short, this activity allows participants to recognize and verbalize how sociocultural norms and life experiences influenced their self-image and self-worth. In addition, by opposing the speeches of the inner critic (oppressive sociocultural) mode with a more affirmative, respectful, and kind view of themselves, they begin to challenge and restructure beliefs and schemas, promoting a shift toward a more compassionate and realistic personal view. At the end of the exercise, therapists may suggest that participants tear up the letters as a way of detaching themselves from the intense and unpleasant emotions associated with this oppressive figure, including those related to their sexual orientation, gender identity, and existence.

Good Parents Exercise: Short Version

Objectives: To build a model of a good caregiver; understand how to adequately meet one's own emotional needs.

Procedure: Therapists start by asking participants to describe, based on what they learned in the previous exercise, what a good caregiver would be like for them. The group can collectively list characteristics and qualities they consider important.

For example, a person who had a loving mother may highlight the importance of a welcoming and sensitive caregiver. Someone who had a strict but didactic father may emphasize the need for gentle boundaries. Therapists guide the conversation so that the model created by the group includes essential elements that meet the five core emotional needs (secure attachment, healthy boundaries, space for autonomy, emotional validation, and play).

Therapists explain that, although the past cannot be changed, each participant can now act as a caregiver for themselves, assuming the role of a healthy adult. This adult, who has been strengthened throughout the sessions, is the figure that welcomes vulnerabilities and meets the needs of the child modes. Even those who did not have adequate caregivers in childhood can learn to meet their emotional needs in a warm and organized way.

The model built in the group reflects an ideal caregiver who, in fact, would be effective and capable of meeting a person's emotional needs well. It is important that each participant personalizes this model, making it good enough for themselves and their child modes. Therapists can highlight that a good caregiver is a genuine figure, capable of rescuing healthy behaviors learned in the past and adapting what was lacking. Even imperfect caregivers may have contributed positive aspects, which can be recognized and incorporated into the personal model.

Each group participant can take some time to try to visualize themselves with this caregiver, recording on paper the characteristics that make them up. They can also list which of their five needs have been met throughout life and which could be better cared for in the present and future—these will be their main focus.

Feedback and Action Plan

Therapists ask for feedback on the session, highlighting the importance of keeping core emotional needs in mind. This practice helps participants take care of their emotions both in the therapeutic environment and in their daily routines. Thus, everyone will always have an effective tool for emotional regulation and self-care in the face of difficulties and obstacles.

To further this goal, the action plan is introduced. The objective is for members to continue finding and defining their role as caregivers for themselves in adult life. At home, they can observe what they already do well and what they still need to develop to fully meet their emotional needs. Based on this, each participant should set up to three simple goals (e.g., clean the house twice a week, floss daily, respond to more text messages from friends). These goals serve to direct and intentionally expand self-care throughout the week.

Action plan: Define up to three simple self-care goals to be accomplished throughout the week, focusing on meeting one's own emotional needs.

Appendices and materials needed for Session 5
– Summary of the five core emotional needs (Appendix V)

Further Reading

Cardoso, B. L. A., Lima, A. F. A., Costa, F. R. M., Loose, C., Liu, X., & Fabris, M. A. (2024). Sociocultural implications in the development of early maladaptive schemas in adolescents belonging to sexual and gender minorities. *International Journal of Environmental Research and Public Health, 21*(8). https://doi.org/10.3390/ijerph21080971

Cardoso, B. L. A., Paim, K., Catelan, R. F., & Liebross, E. H. (2022). Minority stress and the inner critic/oppressive sociocultural schema mode among sexual and gender minorities. *Current Psychology, 42*, 19991–19999. https://doi.org/10.1007/s12144-022-03086-y

Farrell, J. M., & Shaw, I. A. (2020). Creative use of mode dialogues with the vulnerable child and dysfunctional critic modes. In J. S. Heath & M. Startup (Eds.), *Creative methods in schema therapy: Advances and innovation in clinical practice*. Routledge.

Farrell, J. M., & Shaw, I. A. (2018). *Experiencing schema therapy from the inside out: A self-practice/self-reflection workbook for therapists*. The Guilford Press.

Farrell, J. M., & Shaw, I. A. (2012). *Group schema therapy for borderline personality disorder: A step-by-step treatment manual with patient workbook*. Wiley-Blackwell.

Rafaeli, E., Bernstein, D. P., & Young, J. (2011). *Schema therapy*. Routledge.

van der Wijngaart, R. (2021). *Imagery rescripting: Theory and practice*. Pavilion Publishing & Media.

Young, J. E., Klosko, J. S., & Weishaar, M. E. (2003). *Schema therapy: A practitioner's guide*. Guilford Press.

Part II
Intermediate Sessions: Changing My Way of Thinking, Acting, and Feeling Through the Integration of Schema Therapy and Affirmative Therapy

Chapter 7
"I Think, Therefore I (Do Not) Criticize Myself": Cognitive Strategies for Coping with the Inner Critic (Oppressive Sociocultural) Mode

In the sixth session, the central focus is to address and combat the inner critic (oppressive sociocultural) mode through cognitive strategies. The therapists guide the participants on a journey of thought restructuring, using techniques such as Socratic questioning, the identification of cognitive distortions, and the creation of a "well-being box"—a tool similar to a coping card—to intervene cognitively. These strategies empower group members to identify negative thoughts and self-judgments related to their sexual orientation and/or gender identity, allowing them to challenge these distortions and build a healthier and more realistic perspective about themselves (Table 7.1).

Initial Exercise: Mindful Breathing

Objectives: To emotionally regulate the participants to start the session and promote relaxation.

Procedure: This practice aims to provide relaxation and stimulate the participants' mental presence to the current moment, contributing to reducing emotional activation in subsequent activities. For this, the group is instructed to adopt a meditative mindset, with eyes closed or half-closed, in a comfortable position. The narration of the practice is conducted by one of the therapists.

Activity narration: "Today we will start our session with a breathing exercise, to be well, attentive, and present during our meeting. To start, close your eyes or leave them half-closed. Pay attention to the environment around you: sounds, smells. Whatever comes, any sensation is welcome. Stay attentive to these observations for a few minutes. (Pause). Now, turn your attention to your body. Notice the temperature, pressure, touch. The weight of the body against the chair. (Pause). Perceive any bodily sensation calmly and curiously, even if it is just an itch. Observe each aspect of your body for a few minutes. (Pause). Finally, let's direct our attention to the

B. L. A. Cardoso, A. C. G. Braga, *The PRISMAS Group Therapy Handbook*,
https://doi.org/10.1007/978-3-031-91809-4_7

Table 7.1 Session activities and estimated duration

Activity/Intervention	Estimated duration
Initial exercise: Mindful breathing	15 min
Review of the action plan	15 min
Understanding and addressing the inner critic (oppressive sociocultural) mode	35 min
Discussion about thought traps and coping mechanisms	35 min
Feedback and action plan (beginning of the creation of the Well-being box)	20 min

breathing. Let's stay for a longer time observing it. Notice the breathing cycles, perceive the air entering and leaving through your nose. Try to breathe more slowly, releasing your tongue from the roof of the mouth and relaxing your shoulders. (Pause). After a few minutes noticing the breath passing through your nose, and notice how your chest moves as you breathe. Allow it to move gently as the air rises and falls through the throat. (Pause). Rest your attention for some time on these sensations. (Pause). Now go to your belly and feel its movement, inflating and deflating, like a balloon, as you inhale and exhale. (Pause). Observe the sensations of inhaling and exhaling in this region of the body. (Pause). Finally, after paying attention to our breathing, we will gradually return attention to the environment around, leaving behind the meditation. (Pause). Start to gently move your arms and legs. (Pause). When you are ready, open your eyes."

Application tips: The same guidelines for the use of imagery, such as maintaining care with the tone of voice and the rhythm of speech, also apply to relaxation and mindfulness practices. After finishing the practice, it is important that the therapists communicate to participants that the session may be emotionally more intense, but that they will not be alone and will have a safe place to deal with the challenges. The topic of the inner critic (oppressive sociocultural) mode will be resumed, with more challenging techniques, suitable for the group's preparation, which has already started strengthening the healthy adult in the previous meeting. The co-therapist will be available to offer individual support to any participant who feels uncomfortable during the practices throughout the session. It is essential that everyone feels protected and welcomed, ready to face the next steps. Verbally reinforce that the therapists believe in the participants' ability to experience these practices and express pride in the progress achieved so far.

Action Plan Review

Therapists ask for volunteers among the participants to share their experiences in carrying out the planned self-care actions for the week. They also ask if there were difficulties in maintaining these actions and explore the possible obstacles faced. During the discussion, they seek to offer explanations and alternatives, such as dividing the desired behavior into smaller steps to facilitate the creation of a habit. In addition, the therapists explain the process of solidifying a new behavior: "To create consistency in something new, we need two skills: discipline and self-compassion. Discipline involves organizing the habit — setting a fixed time in the day (reducing the chances of giving up or procrastinating), facilitating the start (e.g., leaving exercise clothes ready next to the bed if you want to train in the morning), and having short-, medium-, and long-term reinforcers (clear rewards associated with the habit). Self-compassion is essential for accepting the inevitable failures (like forgetting or losing motivation at the beginning) and persisting despite them. It also involves valuing small starts, even with low frequency or intensity, because the most important thing is consistency."

Even if the participants have only performed one self-care action, this attempt should already be validated and encouraged. The goal of the activity is to motivate participants to start strengthening their healthy affirmative adult also outside of the sessions.

Understanding and Knowing the Inner Critic (Oppressive Sociocultural) Mode

At this stage, therapists discuss important aspects of this mode: its triggers, origins, similarities with reference figures, sensations caused, among others.

Objectives: To identify the stimuli that activate the inner critic (oppressive sociocultural) mode.

Procedure: The therapists introduce the topic explaining that, although in session 3 a experiential activity was carried out to visualize the inner critic (oppressive sociocultural) mode, the focus now is to deepen the understanding of how it works and how to identify it. The discussion can start with examples brought by the participants themselves in previous sessions. Guiding questions:

1. In what situations have you noticed the inner critic (oppressive sociocultural) mode arise? Are there contexts where it appears more frequently?
2. When you think about the inner critic (oppressive sociocultural) mode, does it resemble the speech of any significant figure in your life (e.g., caregiver, religious figure)?
3. How do you feel when you are in this mode? Are there emotions or physical sensations that can signal to you that it's been activated?
4. Is there any character from a series or movie that represents this mode well?
5. Have you noticed this mode more present at any particular stage of your life? When was the first time you noticed this pattern?
6. In childhood or adolescence, do you remember someone who was very critical or were there any social expectations that caused this feeling (e.g., "it's wrong to like someone of the same gender")?

Important considerations: It is essential to adopt a welcoming and attentive attitude, validating the emotions of the participants during the discussion. Encourage participation, including those who tend to be more reserved, without pressuring or crossing boundaries. Consider that the topic can be sensitive and activating for some participants, requiring care, empathy, and attention. Understanding the common stimuli and responses to the inner critic (oppressive sociocultural) mode helps the participants to identify it more clearly, promoting refined self-monitoring. This facilitates the perception that this mode arose as an internal part, but does not define who they are. This separation reduces identification with automatic thoughts, relieving guilt and anguish associated with these cognitions.

Discussion About Thought Traps and Coping Modes

Continuing the previous discussion, therapists now direct attention to the content of the thoughts that participants usually experience when the inner critic (oppressive sociocultural) mode is active. From the examples raised in the previous activity, therapists seek to associate them with the so-called thought traps. This strategy allows a personalized approach, contextualizing theoretical concepts and facilitating their assimilation by the participants. To introduce the concept of cognitive distortions, therapists can explain that thought traps are ways of thinking that are unhealthy, which often cause suffering and are influenced by each person's life history, as well as by the values and beliefs internalized over time. A simple metaphor can illustrate the concept:

> We all see the world through lenses with specific colors. When we are in love, for example, we use rose-colored lenses, which make us see everything in a more optimistic and vibrant way. In difficult times, it's as if we put on gray lenses, which make everything look gloomier and more lifeless. In addition to these temporary lenses, our life history shapes the permanent lenses we use. Imagine, for example, if I brought a chocolate for each of you. Most could be happy and grateful. However, a person with lactose intolerance could react differently, perhaps with sadness or discomfort. The stimulus is the same — the chocolate — but the lenses of each of us determine how we perceive it. Thus, these "glasses help us at times, but they can also trap us in harmful patterns — the pitfalls of our own thoughts.

After the explanation, the therapists present a list of thought traps. This can be displayed on a board or in slides, with space for notes. In Table 7.2, there is a description of each trap (cf. Beck, 2020), offering examples that resonate with the group's experience.

The focus in this exercise is not for participants to memorize all the traps or to be quickly able to identify them in their lives. A brochure containing this summary should be given to each one by the co-therapist (see Appendix VI). The goal of the exercise is to identify how thoughts can follow unhealthy patterns, both in the inner critic (oppressive sociocultural) mode and in the inner critic modes in general. The most important thing is for participants to start questioning the content of their thoughts; it is not necessary for them to memorize the terms or concepts, as an

Table 7.2 List and examples of thought traps

• *Personalization*: A form of distorted thinking that involves attributing external events to oneself, as if the blame for something broad was your responsibility. For example: "I am to blame for my family's suffering because I am gay/lesbian/bisexual/trans." imagining that any sadness or discomfort of loved ones is your fault and your gender identity and/or sexual orientation, ignoring the sociocultural factors of prejudice against sexual and gender diversity
• *Catastrophizing (fortune telling)*: A form of distorted thinking that involves expecting the worst possible scenario will occur, often exaggerating the consequences of a situation. For example: "I will be extremely rejected by my friends and family and will be unable to fully live my sexuality as an LGBTQIA+ person." this thought predicts a catastrophic negative outcome in relation to the person's personal future, due to their sexual orientation and/or gender identity. This interpretation may ignore the friends who would really support them and/or the new friendships that could be built more aligned with who they really are
• *"All-or-nothing" thinking*: A form of distorted thinking that involves seeing situations in an extremist way (black or white), without recognizing their nuances. For example: "If I don't get the highest grade, I'm a complete failure. Because I am a person of the LGBTQIA+ community, I need to compensate in some way." this attitude ignores the possibility that there are many levels of success and failure and that a grade below perfection does not mean total failure. Also, it is a trap by diminishing one's own achievements in view of their gender identity and/or sexual orientation.
• *Disqualifying or discounting the positive*: A form of distorted thinking that involves rejecting or minimizing positive experiences, attributing them to luck, coincidence, or external circumstances, instead of recognizing one's own merit or positive qualities. For example: "I got the job, but it was only because of the diversity campaign, not because I was especially qualified." this perspective disregards the effort, skills, or qualifications that may have contributed to success, attributing it entirely to external factors
• *Emotional reasoning*: A form of distorted thinking that involves letting emotions dictate conclusions, without objective analysis. For example: "People even say that I'm interesting, but I feel inadequate and uninteresting." the person, in this case, may be stuck to their own perception and not identify that this is just a thought that does not correspond with reality
• *Labeling*: A form of distorted thinking that involves generalizing mistakes or specific behaviors as absolute definitions about oneself or others. For example: "I'm bisexual, so I need to have a very active love life." this thought has an inadequate idea of what bisexuality is. It is common for people to confuse concepts such as gender roles (acting in a more socially feminine or masculine way), sexual behavior (having few or many partners), and sexual orientation, although one thing does not necessarily relate to the other
• *Magnification/Minimization*: A form of distorted thinking that involves amplifying negative aspects and diminishing the positives in a situation, especially when they relate to one's own achievements. For example: "I only got the promotion because no one else wanted the job. I made several mistakes in the process." it is common for sexual and gender minorities to discredit their own achievements and have lower self-esteem than average, even though they are competent. Therefore, they may minimize their qualities and success, focusing on the negative points

(continued)

Table 7.2 (continued)

• *Mental filter (selective abstraction)*: A form of distorted thinking that involves focusing only on the negative of a situation, ignoring the positive. For example: "Since I couldn't have a good date [even though I've had other good dates], this means that I am a terrible person." this statement ignores several positive aspects that have already occurred and filters the information in a way that leaves only a view that one is a terrible person due to the last date
• *Tunnel vision*: A form of distorted thinking that involves seeing only the negative aspects, ignoring alternatives, usually with a pessimistic bias. For example: "My friend didn't greet me properly; he must be disappointed with me or angry." in this type of thinking, the person may ignore the other possible alternatives for this situation, such as the friend being busy or going through personal problems, for example
• *Mind reading*: A form of distorted thinking that involves assuming that you know what others they are thinking. For example: "He didn't respond to my 'good morning'; he must find me annoying." the best way to know what other people are thinking is to ask them what they are thinking. By assuming that we know what they are thinking, we can make mistakes in thoughts that are not compatible with reality
• *Overgeneralization*: A form of distorted thinking that involves turning an isolated experience into a broad rule. For example: "Since I was rejected by this person I'm getting to know, no one else will find me interesting and/or want anything to do with me." in this way of thinking, there is an unfair generalization that all relationships and/or encounters will be bad and that no one will be interested in the person
• *"Should" and "must" statements*: A form of distorted thinking that involves imposing rigid expectations on oneself or others. For example: "I should handle everything alone; asking for help is weakness." this way of thinking ignores that social contact and asking for help are part of the human experience. Asking for help does not make a person a failure, but is a common human experience for everyone

excess of information is not effective. The focus is for group members to understand the reasoning behind cognitive traps, learn to pay attention to them, and understand why they are relevant.

Next, the therapists highlight the importance of reflecting on the various ways of dealing with criticisms or challenging and painful thoughts. Then, three main coping styles are presented, along with a fourth healthier option, which can be formulated together by the participants and therapists. Using examples of distorted thoughts offered by the participants themselves, the therapist will ask them to think about different reactions, healthy or not, that they could have had at that moment.

Example of narration: "Let's take the example of Peter. He said that he realized, over the weeks, that he often thinks: 'I can't hold hands with my boyfriend; we are gay, and that is strange and inappropriate' when he is with Caio, his partner. We concluded together that seeing himself as inappropriate and strange is a thought trap, as there is nothing wrong with Peter's sexual orientation or his relationship with another man. As we saw in the previous examples, this type of thought can be a 'labeling,' as Peter is summing up his entire existence in his own sexual orientation, in addition to attributing a negative label to it, which is quite unfair. Peter, can we use your example again to talk about how we can react to a thought like this?" (Upon participant's acceptance). "Thank you very much for contributing with us again! It is very kind of you and valuable for us all. So, let's think together: how do you think a person could react to this thought? Does anyone have a suggestion? If you could share personal experiences in dealing with thoughts like this, it would be very enriching!"

Based on the group's suggestions, the therapists complement with other examples and, finally, present the concept of the three main coping styles. They are:

Overcompensation: A coping style that occurs when a person reacts excessively to a situation, trying to overcome a perception of weakness or failure. This can lead to excessive efforts in certain areas as a way to compensate for insecurity. For example, the person, in the situation described by Peter, could frequent places that are not safe or comfortable for the population of SGM and argue aggressively if he noticed someone looking at the couple. In this scenario, he would put himself at risk by trying to overcome his insecurity and fear through overcompensation.

Avoidance: A coping style that involves running away from or denying problems instead of facing them directly. It can be a defense mechanism to avoid the pain or discomfort associated with a difficult situation. For example, the person could avoid holding his partner's hand in public, using excuses whenever Caio asked to express affection, such as claiming that his hands were sweaty or that he did not like physical contact.

Surrender: A coping style that occurs when a person passively accepts a situation, often feeling that nothing can be done to change it. This can lead to feelings of helplessness and hopelessness. For example, this same individual could internalize the idea that he is indeed a strange and inappropriate person, which could generate internal conflicts and with his own partner.

These coping styles illustrate different ways of reacting to challenging situations. Overcompensation can lead to excessive and possibly harmful efforts; avoidance can result in the denial or escape of problems; and surrender can generate a passive acceptance, without any attempt to change. Each of these strategies has its own implications and can be more or less useful depending on the context and situation. For example, in cases where there is a real risk of suffering a homo/bi/transphobic attack, avoidance can be a temporary strategy to avoid physical and emotional harm. On the other hand, discussing and setting boundaries in safe environments can be important in promoting functional behavior. Thus, coping styles should be evaluated considering the specific context.

Therapists can encourage the group to think of a healthy strategy to deal with challenging thoughts. In this case, perhaps Peter could talk to his partner, share his insecurities, and allow Caio to welcome and reassure him.

Application tips: To prevent the exercise from extending excessively and compromising the flow of the meeting, it is recommended to work with a maximum of 2 or 3 examples, informing this in advance to the participants. In this way, the discussion can be deep, but organized. Therapists should be attentive to ensure space for all participants, alternating volunteers to prevent the focus fall only on one or two people. This requires careful observation of their own emotions and thoughts on the part of the therapists, in order to identify and mitigate the natural tendency to connect more with some group members. It is important that the therapist actively seek to involve all participants, including those who show greater avoidance.

Feedback, Action Plan, and Beginning of the Creation of the Well-Being Box

Just like in previous meetings, therapists should request feedback on the session and participants can share what they learned in the session. This time, unlike previous sessions, the task begins to be performed even during the session. This approach aims to slow down the pace, especially considering that the previous activity may have been emotionally activating. Thus, it seeks to help participants return to a more balanced emotional state before closing.

The "well-being box" is introduced as a concrete resource to assist group members in defusing critical and negative thoughts, embracing their vulnerabilities and practicing self-care. It is a collection, physical or digital, of positive reminders and stimuli that serve as an emotional support tool. During the session, each participant begins to assemble their own box, which can include items such as recorded audios with inspiring messages, notes stored on the cell phone, photos of happy moments, and pieces of paper with alternative and affirmative thoughts. A practical suggestion is to distribute shoe boxes, which can serve as a "self-care toolbox" to store these items. If this is not feasible, digital alternatives, such as creating a WhatsApp group with yourself, a folder on Google Drive, or other similar resources, are also possibilities.

The task is continued at home, with participants being encouraged to add more elements that promote their well-being. Special emphasis is given to the inclusion of references that represent people, characters, and symbols of the LGBTQIA+ community. Another interesting possibility is that the therapist and/or co-therapist can record an affirmative voice message for the participants to save on their technological devices. This allows a greater connection with the therapists throughout the week. This intervention aims to offer participants a tangible and personalized tool for use in times of crisis, stress, or distress. The box works as an accessible resource filled with stimuli capable of rescuing the participants from a negative mental state. By associating visual, auditory, and textual elements with personal meanings, the box strengthens the sense of positive identity, resilience, and autonomy in managing emotional health. In addition, by including inspiring references from LGBTQIA+ figures, the intervention promotes a feeling of belonging and validation. This approach highlights the importance of creating a welcoming and empowering space, encouraging personal and community growth of the participants.

Action plan: Continue elaborating and revisiting the well-being box during the week.

Appendices and materials needed for Session 6
– Sheets with the list of thought traps to distribute to the participants (Appendix VI)

Reference

Beck, J. S. (2020). *Cognitive behavior therapy: Basics and beyond* (3rd ed.). Guilford Publications.

Further Reading

Cardoso, B. L. A., Lima, A. F. A., Costa, F. R. M., Loose, C., Liu, X., & Fabris, M. A. (2024). Sociocultural implications in the development of early maladaptive schemas in adolescents belonging to sexual and gender minorities. *International Journal of Environmental Research and Public Health, 21*(8). https://doi.org/10.3390/ijerph21080971

Cardoso, B. L. A., Paim, K., Catelan, R. F., & Liebross, E. H. (2022). Minority stress and the inner critic/oppressive sociocultural schema mode among sexual and gender minorities. *Current Psychology, 42*, 19991–19999. https://doi.org/10.1007/s12144-022-03086-y

Farrell, J. M., & Shaw, I. A. (2020). Creative use of mode dialogues with the vulnerable child and dysfunctional critic modes. In J. S. Heath & M. Startup (Eds.), *Creative methods in schema therapy: Advances and innovation in clinical practice*. Routledge.

Farrell, J. M., & Shaw, I. A. (2018). *Experiencing schema therapy from the inside out: A self-practice/self-reflection workbook for therapists*. The Guilford Press.

Farrell, J. M., & Shaw, I. A. (2012). *Group schema therapy for borderline personality disorder: A step-by-step treatment manual with patient workbook*. Wiley-Blackwell.

Rafaeli, E., Bernstein, D. P., & Young, J. (2011). *Schema therapy*. Routledge.

van der Wijngaart, R. (2021). *Imagery rescripting: Theory and practice*. Pavilion Publishing & Media.

Young, J. E., Klosko, J. S., & Weishaar, M. E. (2003). *Schema therapy: A practitioner's guide*. Guilford Press.

Chapter 8
"The Child Who Lives in Me": Welcoming the Child Modes

The seventh session of PRISMAS is dedicated to understanding and welcoming the child modes (happy, angry, vulnerable, and impulsive/undisciplined). During this session, therapists use a limited reparenting approach, welcoming the modes and meeting core emotional needs appropriately. By acting as models of good caregivers for the group, therapists assist participants in identifying and understanding their own child modes, promoting the connection of their emotions with these specific modes. In this way, participants are prepared to recognize and meet their core emotional needs in different contexts of their lives (Table 8.1).

Initial Exercise: Imagery of the Ice Cream Shop to Stimulate the Happy Child

Objectives: To activate the "happy child"mode and start the session in a fun and calm atmosphere.

Procedures: This exercise is based on Farrell and Shaw (2012). The therapist should explain to the participants that they will make an imagery intended to activate a fun and playful side within themselves. It is important to emphasize that they do not need to feel embarrassed or silly—the idea is that the practice is a remembering of pleasant experiences from childhood. If any participant reports not having had many happy moments in their childhood experience, therapists can suggest, precisely, the task of allowing themselves to live childish fun in the present.

Narration of the activity: "Let's start this experiential exercise by closing our eyes again and taking in a deep breath. (Pause). Gradually, bring your attention to the story I'm going to narrate. These days, I won a contest on the Internet to go to an ice cream shop. The winner gets to eat as much ice cream as they want, for free! And it's not just any ice cream shop — it's the tastiest in town. They allowed me to bring some guests, and I chose you, here from the group. We're all going there

B. L. A. Cardoso, A. C. G. Braga, *The PRISMAS Group Therapy Handbook*,
https://doi.org/10.1007/978-3-031-91809-4_8

Table 8.1 Session activities and estimated duration

Activity/Intervention	Estimated duration
Initial exercise: Imagery of the ice cream shop to stimulate the happy child	20 min
Review of the action plan	15 min
Identify, together, the child modes present in oneself	25 min
Imagery rescripting exercise: Rewriting a story	40 min
Feedback and action plan	10 min

together. (Pause) I pick you up by car, passing by each one's house. We happily chat on the way there. (Pause) Eventually, we arrive at the ice cream shop! The space is beautiful, colorful, and it's a sunny and pleasant day. (Pause). We go in, and each person receives a bowl to serve themselves. The attendant informs us that we can choose any flavor we want to try, without any restrictions. There are more than 100 flavors, all delicious. You can decide which ones you will serve yourself, without rush. Look at each one and take the necessary time to decide. (Pause) You put some scoops of ice cream into your bowl. The toppings and fillings are also free! I assembled my ice cream like this (the therapist describes their favorite ice cream). And yours, can you visualize how you assembled it? (Pause) We sit together and start eating. What is the taste of the ice cream? Does it have any particular smell? What does it look like? (Pause). We are all laughing and chatting, while we enjoy our ice cream. (Pause). When you finish the ice cream, you appreciate the last bite in your mouth. Savor this feeling of contentment and joy. (Pause). After some time, I take you home and we go our separate ways. Visualize the end of our ride, slowly. (Pause). Gradually, let the image fade and focus back on your breathing. (Pause). Make small movements in your body, like stretching or moving your hands and feet. (Pause). When you feel ready, open your eyes and return your attention to the present moment."

Review of the Action Plan

At the beginning of the session, therapists can ask participants how their experience was during the week after the previous session, highlighting that they are available to provide support if it was difficult to manage the emotions that arose. Then, they can request that each person share a little of their experience in assembling their well-being box, including the possibility of sharing with the group, if they feel comfortable, some of the objects chosen to compose their kits.

Based on the previous activity, therapists can introduce the idea that the healthy adult, widely discussed in the sessions, has a younger counterpart: the happy child—introduced in the first sessions. While the adult focuses on responsibilities, is organized, and diligently takes care of his chores, the happy child has fun, laughs, and carries lightness. Both modes are important and necessary at different times. The therapist may ask if any participant has brought elements that represent the happy child to their little box, assisting in differentiating between the two modes and their respective activations.

Identify, Together, the Child Modes Present in Oneself

Objective: To facilitate the perception of child modes, including cognitions, sensations, behaviors, and emotions associated with them.

Procedure: At the beginning of the intervention, the therapists remind the group of the concept of child modes. These modes represent different ways of feeling and reacting, with roots in childhood. Memories, emotions, and childhood experiences have a significant influence on the way people perceive and respond to present situations. Because they have been long-established modes that are deeply rooted, they are called "child modes." There are four child modes: angry child, undisciplined/impulsive child, happy child, and vulnerable child (Rafaeli et al., 2011; Young et al., 2003).

In the initial stage of the intervention, the focus is to deepen the discussion about these modes. Each one is explained and analyzed in detail, considering how it manifests in the participants' daily lives. To enrich this reflection, therapists can invite members to remember a recent situation where they felt dominated by one of these modes and to share their experiences with the group. If any participant has difficulty with this self-monitoring, therapists can serve as a model, presenting personal examples of times when they experienced these modes—always respecting professional boundaries and using good judgment in self-disclosures.

In the second stage, attention turns to the stimuli that activate each of the modes. Therapists can explain that certain "triggers" spur reactions, as was discussed in conversations about other modes previously. Similar questions to those in previous sessions can be asked, such as "What thoughts come up? What do you feel?" These questions help participants identify the specific stimuli that lead them to access these emotional states.

The therapist can explore with the group events or situations that can often put them under the influence of these modes. Then, participants are encouraged to explore the personal origins of these modes. This reflection may include dialogues about childhood memories or past experiences that contributed to the formation of the modes. The relationship with significant figures throughout life can also be addressed in this discussion. Table 8.2 briefly describes a summary of the four child modes, according to Paim and Cardoso (2019), Wainer and Rijo (2016), and Young et al. (2003). It is recommended to revisit Session 2 for a more complete understanding of their characteristics, in addition to consulting the corresponding illustrations again before applying this session.

Table 8.2 Understanding child modes

Understanding child modes
Vulnerable child mode: This mode is characterized by painful memories and emotions from childhood, such as fear and insecurity. When activated, the person seeks protection and approval, often feeling excluded or rejected in relationships. When in this mode, the person expresses their needs in a desperate way, with physical and behavioral manifestations that include distress, reassurance seeking, and facial expressions of sadness. Its needs include support, validation, and secure attachment
Undisciplined/impulsive child mode: This mode is characterized by resistance to rules and limits, often rooted in experiences of restriction or lack of limits in childhood. When in this mode, the person can engage in hasty and impulsive behaviors, in search of immediate gratification, potentially putting the person or others at risk. Despite appearing irreverent or defiant, it needs healthy limits to achieve emotional regulation
Angry child mode: This mode is characterized by intense emotions of anger and frustration, often originating from experiences of injustice or emotional abuse in childhood. When in this mode, the person may experience emotional outbursts and aggressive behaviors. They need emotional validation for anger and a safe space to vent their emotions. Physically, this mode can show itself through redness in the cheeks and a feeling of heat
Happy child mode: This mode is characterized by light and joyful feelings, associated with memories of positive moments from childhood. When in this mode, the person may experience feelings of joy, curiosity, and spontaneity, promoting pleasure in simple activities and valuing contentment. People in this mode usually present themselves as smiling and laughing, with an innocent joy. Recognizing this mode is essential to balance the demands of adult life with moments of leisure and happiness

Imagery Rescripting Exercise: Rewriting a Story

Objectives: To apply the model developed in the previous intervention and strengthen the practice of self-care, focusing on the continuation of the work started in Session 5.

Procedure: In this therapeutic activity, participants will be guided into a space for reflection and connection with their emotions, especially those associated with the vulnerable child mode (and, to a lesser extent, the other child modes). The goal is to create an atmosphere of safety and compassion, providing each individual with the opportunity to explore their feelings, understand their origins, and learn to manage them in a healthy way. For this, two models will be used as reference.

Narration of the activity: *For this exercise, let's close our eyes or keep them half-closed, as you prefer. This practice will help us to connect more deeply with our emotions. I will speak more slowly from now on, to facilitate this process. (Pause). Gradually, start breathing slowly and calmly, noticing the natural rhythm of your breath, as you inhale and exhale. (Pause). Gradually, visualize your Safe Place. If you wish, you can also imagine your Protective Bubble surrounding you. This is a space where you can feel completely safe and calm. Here, nothing bad can happen. (Pause). Now, let's listen to some stories that relate to our inner child sides. First, I will share a situation from my own life. Then, I invite a volunteer who feels comfortable to also share a personal story."*

At this point in the exercise, it is interesting for the therapist to share a personal story that is appropriate to the context: neither excessively intimate, nor superficial. The goal is for the story to be somewhat activating from an emotional point of view, to provide a model for the participants, and to stimulate the group's connection with their own experiences. In addition, this approach contributes to humanizing the therapist, strengthening the bond and trust between him and the participants; see Table 8.3.

For this manual, considering the cultural context, the following example can be used (although it is preferable to use a personal story from the therapist themselves): Once, the therapist asked their mother to take them to the bathroom while they were at the mall, looking at Christmas presents. However, she refused, saying that they could wait a little longer, as they would finish shopping soon and go home. They ended up peeing and wetting their pants, which was extremely embarrassing and generated feelings of anger, shame, and betrayal. Even so, the mother scolded them, accusing them of not being able to hold it in and complaining that now they would have to buy new pants, causing additional work and expenses. The therapist was very sad and embarrassed, but waited in silence while the mother bought the new pants, wearing them without saying a word, although they felt deeply helpless inside.

Continuation of the imagery rescripting (from the previous example, with the co-therapist playing the role of acceptance):

Co-therapist: How did you feel in that situation?

Therapist: I wanted to cry, to fight with my mother, all at the same time. I wanted to get out of there and hide.

Co-therapist: How did your mother react, seeing you go through this situation?

Therapist: She was irritated. She said: 'you can never wait. I said we were going home soon! Now I will have to spend more time and money than I had planned'. She acted as if I had thrown a tantrum and was deliberately causing problems.

Co-therapist: What do you think you needed to hear at that moment?

Table 8.3 Narrative for the activity

Farrell and Shaw (2012), in their group for patients with borderline personality disorder, used the following example of a story, which happened with Joan. Here, it is adapted and presented indirectly: "*I will share a memory from my childhood that reveals a lot about my vulnerable child. It was a moment when I needed a loving parent, but unfortunately, I had no one to fill that role. (pause). Imagine yourself observing a store from the outside, through a window that allows you to see everything inside. When I was 6 years old, I was in a small souvenir shop during a family vacation. (pause). I was excited to choose a gift for myself and decided that I wanted a snow globe that fit within my budget. Suddenly, it slipped from my hands and broke. The store owner yelled at me, and my mother, instead of defending me, remained silent. (pause). I was devastated, but I managed to hold back the tears, as I was with family and felt ashamed, afraid of making a scene and causing trouble. (pause). I felt like a bad, lonely, and sad child.*" This story can be used as a reference or even interpreted by the therapist, in case they do not feel ready and free to use a personal situation. As can be noted, Joan's story is emotional, yet simple and light, without crossing therapist–patient boundaries. The situation chosen by the therapist should, preferably, follow this pattern

Therapist: I think just an 'it's okay, these things 'happen, let's look at new pants together?' or 'I'm sorry for yelling at you, I'm a little tired and I got carried away'. Recognizing that I was a good child, I was not to blame for that. She was tired and got stressed - which I understand. But I needed her to admit that to me and help me calm down and deal with the shame.

Co-therapist: I'm sorry about that. Shall we try to rewrite this story? I'm going to tell you some things that I believe a good caregiver could have told you in this situation. You can try to internalize what I just said, as if I were in the scene, talking to you and taking care of your vulnerable child. Is that okay?

Therapist: yes, I can try.

Co-therapist: thank you very much. I would like to say that you are a very mature and careful child, for being so understanding with your mother. She is tired, but that does not give her the right to treat you like this. I want to talk to her now. So, listen up, mother of therapist's name: you need to pay attention to your son's emotions. They are embarrassed. I know you're stressed, but it's unfair to take it out on them, they're just a child. Take them to the bathroom, I'll buy new pants for them to wear and give them to you inside, okay? (to the child) I'm here for you. Both of us will help you calm down, me and your mother - after all, that's the role of adults. Don't be ashamed! Who hasn't peed their pants? It happens to everyone. (Pause). How do you feel hearing this?

Therapist: thank you. I'm still embarrassed, but I'm glad to know that it's not a big deal. That I have someone to count on and that we will solve the problem.

Co-therapist: and what else can we say to them, folks? Would anyone else like to say words of affection and care to the child of therapist's name? ".

Space is given for the group to offer encouragement and care, speaking directly to the therapist's vulnerable child. In this way, participants have the opportunity to put into practice their own models of good caregivers. Then, the process is repeated with one of the participants, who voluntarily shares a personal story, receiving the same support and care from the group. If time allows, more people can share their experiences, or even all participants, if the group is small. This decision is up to the therapists. The experience is concluded with a discussion, in which both the volunteer participant(s) and the others present in the group share how this experience was for them.

Session Feedback and Action Plan Handover

Once again, the therapists ask for feedback about the session from the group members. In this meeting, due to the more activating potential of the task "Rewriting your Story," it is important to maintain a welcoming and caring demeanor. To help decrease emotional activation, it may be interesting, in addition to what was suggested in the previous meeting (attend individually to participants who need support), to return to the ice cream shop activity, recalling the pleasant sensation experienced there for about 5–10 min. This will help to end the session in a lighter and calmer way.

The action plan for the week will consist of reflecting on the imagery made during the session, focusing on continuing to be a good caregiver to oneself—now with a greater understanding and comprehension of the child modes. Each participant will be encouraged to dedicate some time to think about situations from their childhood that may still impact who they are today and that require them to fulfill this role of caregiver for themselves, even if retroactively. This reflection aims to allow participants to explore their feelings and needs associated with the child modes more deeply, and to work on ways to respond to them with compassion, validation, healthy boundaries, and spontaneity. One suggested way to do this is to record in a diary a little of their childhood experiences and emotional needs, offering themselves what they need to feel good in the present. It is worth noting that the task does not consist of performing, alone, new imagery techniques, as this can be activating and even harmful.

Action plan: diary writing exercise (or daily reflection) as a good caregiver for the child modes, continuation of the activity "rewriting a story."

References

Farrell, J. M., & Shaw, I. A. (2012). *Group schema therapy for borderline personality disorder: A step-by-step treatment manual with patient workbook*. Wiley-Blackwell.

Paim, K., & Cardoso, B. L. A. (2019). Modos Esquemáticos Individuais e o Ciclo de Modos Conjugal. In K. Paim & B. L. A. Cardoso (Eds.), *Terapia do Esquema para Casais: Base Teórica e Intervenção*. Artmed.

Wainer, R., & Rijo, D. (2016). O Modelo Teórico: Esquemas Iniciais Desadaptativos, Estilos de Enfrentamento e Modos Esquemáticos. In R. Wainer, K. Paim, R. Erdos, & R. Andriola (Eds.), *Terapia Cognitiva Focada em Esquemas: Integração em Psicoterapia*. Artmed.

Young, J. E., Klosko, J. S., & Weishaar, M. E. (2003). *Schema therapy: A practitioner's guide*. Guilford Press.

Further Reading

Cardoso, B. L. A., Lima, A. F. A., Costa, F. R. M., Loose, C., Liu, X., & Fabris, M. A. (2024). Sociocultural implications in the development of early maladaptive schemas in adolescents belonging to sexual and gender minorities. *International Journal of Environmental Research and Public Health, 21*(8). https://doi.org/10.3390/ijerph21080971

Cardoso, B. L. A., Paim, K., Catelan, R. F., & Liebross, E. H. (2022). Minority stress and the inner critic/oppressive sociocultural schema mode among sexual and gender minorities. *Current Psychology, 42*, 19991–19999. https://doi.org/10.1007/s12144-022-03086-y

Farrell, J. M., & Shaw, I. A. (2020). Creative use of mode dialogues with the vulnerable child and dysfunctional critic modes. In J. S. Heath & M. Startup (Eds.), *Creative methods in schema therapy: Advances and innovation in clinical practice*. Routledge.

Farrell, J. M., & Shaw, I. A. (2018). *Experiencing schema therapy from the inside out: A self-practice/self-reflection workbook for therapists*. The Guilford Press.
Rafaeli, E., Bernstein, D. P., & Young, J. (2011). *Schema therapy*. Routledge.
Shaw, I. A. (2020). Spontaneity and play in schema therapy. In J. S. Heath & M. Startup (Eds.), *Creative methods in schema therapy: Advances and innovation in clinical practice*. Routledge.
van der Wijngaart, R. (2021). *Imagery rescripting: Theory and practice*. Pavilion Publishing & Media.

Chapter 9
"Where Does This Internal Storm Come From? Understanding My Emotions": Emotion-Focused Strategies for Understanding and Regulating Various Modes

In the eighth session of the program, the focus is on the identification of emotions, rather than seeking a deep emotional change, which will be the goal of the next two meetings. For this, playful elements are introduced, such as the use of diaries and the association of feelings with specific colors. The aim is to provide participants with greater clarity about what they are feeling, as well as a deeper understanding of the origin of their emotions and how they relate to their different modes. The identification of emotions is seen as the fundamental first step for subsequent emotional regulation (Table 9.1).

Review of the Action Plan

The review of the action plan is carried out again, with the aim of encouraging its fulfillment. The action plan seeks to promote an internal immersion, encouraging participants to reflect on how they can be good caregivers of themselves, exploring childhood situations that still resonate in the present. The environment should remain welcoming and empathetic, given the potential of the task to evoke deep and intense emotions. The therapists reinforce that they are present as points of support for all participants.

Then, the focus shifts to sharing the experiences of writing in the diary about childhood experiences. Each participant is invited to share their records and how they met their emotional needs in the present. The session explores emotions, especially those associated with child modes, allowing therapists to use this discussion as an opportunity to explain the importance of emotional regulation and connection with one's own feelings for psychological well-being. Although this activity may be uncomfortable, it is part of the process of change. Many people report that, after classic Cognitive Therapy interventions, such as cognitive restructuring, they can "think differently," but they cannot "believe or feel differently." ST, in turn, is

B. L. A. Cardoso, A. C. G. Braga, *The PRISMAS Group Therapy Handbook*,
https://doi.org/10.1007/978-3-031-91809-4_9

Table 9.1 Session activities and estimated duration

Activity/intervention	Estimated duration
Review of the action plan	15 minutes
Identifying emotions: RAIN	30 minutes
Identifying emotions using colors	35 minutes
Imagery exercise: Space of affirmation	30 minutes
Feedback and action plan	10 minutes

innovative by promoting a deeper connection with one's own life story and the impact that these experiences have had, going beyond the change of automatic thoughts.

Identifying Emotions: RAIN

Objectives:To understand and connect with the predominant emotion at the moment; identify the signs of the presence of an emotion.

Procedure:The therapists explain that, often, we confuse thoughts and emotions. It is common to hear phrases like "I thought I was angry!" when in fact the statement communicates a feeling, or "I felt that he hated me," when in reality the statement communicates a thought, not an emotion. In addition, the traditional educational system often does not teach how to identify one's own emotions, something essential for a person to know how to react to their feelings. Emotional disconnection is also connected with social beliefs, such as "boys don't cry" or "girls have to be nice, they can't get angry." This makes it difficult to understand one's own reactions, hindering self-care. The RAIN technique aims to help perceive and name the emotional state of the moment, without judging or avoiding it (Consenza, 2021).

Narration:"Today, we will do an exercise to help you identify your emotions. It will be a good introduction to our meeting, as we will talk about emotions throughout the day. It may seem difficult or strange at first, especially if you are not used to paying attention to your emotions on a daily basis. However, this is crucial for change. More than thinking differently, we need to learn to deal with what we feel, especially with the oldest and deepest pains. To learn to name our emotions, we will use the acronym 'RAIN'. Each letter has a meaning, and the 'N' has two different functions. Let's start by taking on a meditative mindset. I ask you to close your eyes and breathe deeply. (Pause). Let's start with R which stands for Recognize. Notice any sensation, thought, or emotion in you at this moment. Sensations include temperature, pressure, tingling - anything you feel in the body. (Pause). Thoughts are the words, phrases, and images that pass through your mind. Notice what appears while you do this exercise. (Pause). You may feel restless, excited, sad, confused. Emotions are these internal feelings. (Pause). Observe all these internal processes, without focusing excessively on any of them. Notice how they come and go — they all pass. (Pause). Now let's move on to A which stands for Accept. There may be some discomfort in relation to a thought, sensation or emotion. Let's try not to run away from them, just let them be there, without giving them too much attention.

(Pause). You can imagine yourself saying internally: 'Hi [*name of the emotion, thought or sensation*], goodbye [*name of the emotion, thought or sensation*]'. (Pause). Now, for I which stands for Investigate, bring your focus to the most present emotion at this moment, or the one that you felt the most within the last week. Notice the thoughts and sensations associated with it. (Pause). Give it a name, like 'anger', 'anxiety', 'fear'. If possible, focus on a more uncomfortable emotion, which might be not so comfortable to let yourself feel. (Pause). The first N is for Nurture. Imagine offering yourself what you need to deal with this emotion. You might place your hand on your heart or hug yourself, bringing physical comfort. (Pause). Bring to mind a figure of care and affection, who can tell you what you need to hear at this moment. Stay focused on those words. (Pause). Finally, let's let these images go, with our mind fading to black. The last N is for Non-Identification, that is, realizing that we are not any of these internal events. Notice your breathing, letting thoughts, sensations and emotions go. (Pause). Start making small movements with your body, stretching or moving your hands and feet. (Pause). When you're ready, open your eyes and return to our present space."

After the completion of the exercise, the therapists ask the participants not to immediately share which emotion they perceived as most present during the activity. Instead, the therapists welcome and listen to the general experiences of the exercise, without going into specific details yet, moving directly to the color task, as a natural continuation of the RAIN process.

Identifying Emotions Using Colors

Objectives:Based on Farrell and Shaw (2012), this exercise aims to help the participant understand their own emotions and perceive the emotional fluctuations throughout the meeting.

Procedure:For this activity, participants sit on the floor, forming a circle, with various colored sheets or cards arranged in the center. The therapists start by asking the participants to suggest what each color reminds them of emotionally. For example, a color can evoke feelings of calmness, joy, sadness, etc. This helps to establish a connection between colors and the emotions associated with them. Next, the therapists clarify that, to facilitate the exercise, a specific reference will be used to guide the association of colors with emotions. The colors will be grouped according to widely recognized emotional categories, such as:

Red: anger, frustration, or any other hot emotion in this sense.
Yellow: happiness, joy, fun, pleasure.
Blue: sadness, discouragement, fatigue.
Purple: fear, tension, and apprehension.
Brown: overload, confusion.
Green: disgust, discomfort.
White: tranquility, peace, comfort.

The therapists explain that now the focus is for each participant to select the color that represents the emotion they felt most during the week and that they chose to focus on during the RAIN. It's okay if more than one person chooses the same color. In a clockwise direction, each person says the emotion they felt, how they perceived it in their body and in their thoughts, and why they felt this way during the week. The therapists can follow the same five questions:

1. What color did you choose and how did this emotion appear in your life this week?
2. How did you perceive this emotion in your body?
3. What thoughts appeared in relation to it or before it?
4. What behaviors or impulses did this emotion generate for you?
5. What did this emotion try to communicate to you? What can you learn from it?

In the meantime, the co-therapist notes what each person chose. This exercise should be revisited at the end of the session, after the action plan is reviewed—the participants will choose a new color at this moment, after going through the day's interventions. From this, the therapists analyze if there was an emotional change by asking the following questions:

1. Did your color change?
2. What might have happened during the meeting that caused your color to change?
3. If it didn't change, what made you stay in this emotional state?
4. What emotional needs do you have at this moment and how might this emotion be pointing to it?

Imagery Exercise: Space of Affirmation

Objectives: To connect the group; generate empathy and acceptance among members.

Procedure: A participant, voluntarily, is encouraged to share a challenging situation in which the inner critic (oppressive sociocultural) mode was activated. The rest of the group is invited to participate in the mental image, one by one, with the aim of supporting and holding space for this participant and their experiences. The activity seeks to combat the inner critic (oppressive sociocultural) mode, protect the vulnerable child, and strengthen the connection and sense of belonging to the group. The presence and attention of the therapists are essential to guide the experience and provide emotional support, whenever necessary.

Activity narration: "For our next intervention, we need a volunteer. This person will sit facing me in this exercise. Meanwhile, the others can find a comfortable position in their chairs and, if they want to connect more with the experience, they can close their eyes or keep them half-closed. Breathe slowly for a few moments, feeling each inhale and exhale.

Today, we are going to work together to support one of our colleagues in a challenging moment. I ask that you open up emotionally and be present for each other.

Now, I ask the participant who chose to share with us—and I thank you for your kindness and courage—to remember a recent event that was emotionally activating, like a day when you criticized yourself or felt bad about yourself. Can you describe to me what it was like? Try, if possible, to provide details. I and your colleagues will try to imagine what it was like to be there, experiencing the experience with you. (*The volunteer describes the scene*)

Can you tell me how you felt? Did any specific sensation arise in your body? Where did this sensation appear? What did you think at that moment? (*The volunteer answers the questions, which are asked in a paused and sequential manner*)

Thank you, [*participant's name*]. Now, try to bring to mind the earliest memory you have of feeling this same way. Similar thoughts, emotions, and sensations. Let this memory come naturally, without forcing yourself. Take the time you need to remember. (Pause). Can you describe in detail this scene, as if you were experiencing it now? (*Pause for the volunteer to narrate the old scene*).

Thank you for sharing. I imagine it was a difficult situation for you. I'm glad you felt comfortable sharing it with us—this is very valuable for us. Can you tell me a few more details, if you can, about this situation? How old were you? Who were you with? What was the environment like? What do you remember feeling and thinking in this scene? (*The volunteer answers the questions, which are asked in a paused and sequential manner*)

Now, I'm going to ask you to imagine that we can interrupt this scene in time. Everything freezes, except for your child version, so young and vulnerable. A new character will enter this situation.

Note:There are three possible options for who leads this exercise: The therapist themselves, the healthy adult of the volunteer, or the caregiver of that time can nurture the necessary core emotional needs during the imagery rescripting process. The options are progressively more powerful, but also more emotionally activating. The choice should be made carefully, considering the volunteer, the narrated scene, and the perceived emotionality. This figure, then, seeks to speak directly to the child, in the first person, meeting the present emotional need—for example, combating the inner critic (oppressive sociocultural) mode.

Finally, I invite the rest of the group to join this imagined space and offer support in holding space for our colleague and their experiences. Say what you felt listening to the details of your colleague's experience, one at a time, without rushing. (*The therapist allows the participants to speak and interact in a positive and compassionate way*).

Here, we are creating a sense of belonging and mutual understanding. Thank you for holding space for our colleague. Gradually, I ask that everyone start to breathe slowly, paying attention to the air that passing through your nose, letting the mental image fade. (Pause). Gradually, we will bring our awareness back to the present, taking with us the sensations of compassion and connection.

I want to thank everyone for their participation, openness, and courage. This is a profound and meaningful practice, and it is an honor to be here with you."

The activity seeks to create a sense of community and companionship among the participants. It is important that the co-therapist is attentive to the volunteer (as well as to the rest of the group) during the session, being able to offer individual support if additional welcome is needed after the sharing.

Application tips: Although the written narration does not include spacing between questions, the ideal is that the practice develops in the form of dialogue. Ask, at most, one or two questions at a time, waiting for the participant's response without interrupting their reasoning. In this way, the dialogue will flow naturally, avoiding emotional disconnections or unnecessary haste.

Feedback and Action Plan

The closing of the session is followed by a moment for feedback. Therapists should always encourage the open and honest expression of emotions and thoughts at this stage. The session's action plan aims to consolidate experiential experiences through a creative emotion tracker. This resource facilitates the recognition and recording of emotions by participants, promoting greater emotional awareness. Participants should be instructed to record their emotions daily, in the same way they did in the color practice. They can choose to simply note the most felt emotions or, more visually, color a square with the color corresponding to the predominant emotion of each day.

The therapists encourage the creativity of the participants, adapting the plan to their individual routines. If there are difficulties in fulfilling the tasks, it is important to have a conversation to identify ways to contextualize the activities in their lives and reduce possible obstacles. For example, someone who is not in the habit of taking notes can, initially, reflect on the most felt emotions of the week before the next weekly meeting. This adaptation can be a starting point to creating the habit of participating in the proposed tasks. Finally, the color activity should be performed again at the end of the next session, after reviewing the action plan, reinforcing the process of recognition and emotional expression.

Action plan: Creative tracking of emotions (recording of emotions throughout the week, using the color activity to facilitate the process) (Table 9.2).

Table 9.2 Example of emotion tracking record with colors

Date	Most felt emotion	Color[a]	Reflections about it
09/13/2024	Sadness	Blue	"I felt very sad this day, as I was procrastinating a lot and realized that I put off doing my tasks"
09/14/2024	Joy	Yellow	"It was a calm and enjoyable day, as I managed to handle my tasks. I realized that having an organized day greatly helps my mood"

[a] If the participant chooses to record by colors (as per the colors presented during the session). It can also be illustrated by other creative resources (e.g., songs, seasons, etc.)

Appendices and materials needed for Session 8
– Cut out color cards for the mood activity – Sheets with example of the Emotion Tracker (Appendix VII)

References

Consenza, R. M. (2021). *Neurociência e Mindfulness: meditação, equilíbrio emocional e redução do estresse*. Artmed.

Farrell, J. M., & Shaw, I. A. (2012). *Group schema therapy for borderline personality disorder: A step-by-step treatment manual with patient workbook.* Wiley-Blackwell.

Further Reading

Cardoso, B. L. A., Lima, A. F. A., Costa, F. R. M., Loose, C., Liu, X., & Fabris, M. A. (2024). Sociocultural implications in the development of early maladaptive schemas in adolescents belonging to sexual and gender minorities. *International Journal of Environmental Research and Public Health, 21*(8). https://doi.org/10.3390/ijerph21080971

Cardoso, B. L. A., Paim, K., Catelan, R. F., & Liebross, E. H. (2022). Minority stress and the inner critic/oppressive sociocultural schema mode among sexual and gender minorities. *Current Psychology, 42*, 19991–19999. https://doi.org/10.1007/s12144-022-03086-y

Farrell, J. M., & Shaw, I. A. (2018). *Experiencing schema therapy from the inside out: A self-practice/self-reflection workbook for therapists*. The Guilford Press.

Farrell, J. M., & Shaw, I. A. (2020). Creative use of mode dialogues with the vulnerable child and dysfunctional critic modes. In J. S. Heath & M. Startup (Eds.), *Creative methods in schema therapy: Advances and innovation in clinical practice*. Routledge.

Paim, K., & Cardoso, B. L. A. (2019). Modos Esquemáticos Individuais e o Ciclo de Modos Conjugal. In K. Paim & B. L. A. Cardoso (Eds.), *Terapia do Esquema para Casais: Base Teórica e Intervenção*. Artmed.

Rafaeli, E., Bernstein, D. P., & Young, J. (2011). *Schema therapy*. Routledge.

Shaw, I. A. (2020). Spontaneity and play in schema therapy. In J. S. Heath & M. Startup (Eds.), *Creative methods in schema therapy: Advances and innovation in clinical practice*. Routledge.

van der Wijngaart, R. (2021). *Imagery rescripting: Theory and practice*. Pavilion Publishing & Media.

Young, J. E., Klosko, J. S., & Weishaar, M. E. (2003). *Schema therapy: A practitioner's guide*. Guilford Press.

Chapter 10
"Allowing Myself a New Way of Feeling": Experiential Strategies for Coping with the Inner Critic (Oppressive Sociocultural) Mode

The ninth session focuses on emotional change related to the inner critic (oppressive sociocultural) mode. At this stage, experiential techniques are applied, such as the use of imagery and chairwork exercises, with the aim of allowing a deep exploration of the origins and influences of this mode in the participants' lives. Through these practices, participants are guided to recognize their own reactions and emotional responses, seeking ways to balance them more consciously in everyday life. The process promotes a clearer understanding of emotional dynamics and facilitates the construction of strategies to deal with them in a healthy way (Table 10.1).

Initial Exercise: "Relief Balloon"

Objectives: based on Farrell and Shaw (2012), this exercise aims to promote emotional regulation and engage the self-efficacy of the group participants.

Procedure: This activity uses balloons to address feelings of pressure and discomfort (referred to as "stagnation") within a group. The therapist begins by validating the participants' emotions and identifying where they perceive these sensations in their bodies. The therapists lead a collective discussion about these experiences, exploring similarities and differences among group members. The group can discuss which emotions are associated with these experiences, what caused the discomfort in the week, and in what ways they perceive pressure.

Next, the therapist distributes balloons to the participants, instructing them to blow into them as if they were transferring their feelings of frustration, anger, sadness, pain, tension, and the pressure and discomfort causing situations of that week. After filling the balloons, the participants hold them without tying them, symbolizing the intention to release the pressure and discomfort, rather than to hold them in. Then, following a countdown conducted by the therapist, the balloons are released simultaneously. This practice aims to encourage the relief of psychological

B. L. A. Cardoso, A. C. G. Braga, *The PRISMAS Group Therapy Handbook*,
https://doi.org/10.1007/978-3-031-91809-4_10

Table 10.1 Session activities and estimated duration

Activity/intervention	Estimated duration
Initial exercise: "Relief balloon"	20 minutes
Review of the action plan	15 minutes
Emotional understanding of schema modes	30 minutes
Chairwork technique using balloons: combating the inner critic (oppressive sociocultural) mode	45 minutes
Feedback and action plan	10 minutes

suffering, the replacement of unpleasant emotions with healthier ones, and the experience of a moment of group fun. The therapist may suggest that the participants keep a memory of this experience throughout the session and, if they wish, keep the balloon as a physical reminder of their ability to overcome unpleasant feelings.

Narration: "I invite all of you to join me in this activity that will help us explore and relieve the sensation of pressure and discomfort. First, let's talk about where you perceive these sensations in your bodies. Is it some pressure or feelings of heaviness? What other physical sensation appears? Does it affect your breathing? Does it generate or take away energy? What caused this sensation over the last week? Was there any trigger? What other emotions arose from this? (*The therapist asks the questions sequentially and paused, listening carefully to the group's responses*).

Now, I want each of you to take a balloon from the co-therapist. Blow into it some of the pressure and discomfort we discussed—frustration, anger, sadness, anxiety, memories of stress from the week, whatever comes to mind. Fill the balloon, but do not tie it. Raise your arms and hold the balloons above your head. On the count of three, we will release them. Ready? One, two, three! (*The balloons fly around the room*).

See how this simple action brought some relief? It is important to remember that we can replace these heavy feelings with something light. What positive feelings did you have when you saw the balloons flying? How was it to realize all of us were performing this activity together? Did blowing bring any sense of calmness? Share with me what you felt in this experience!"

Review of the Action Plan

In the review of the action plan, briefly, the therapist focuses on the Creative Tracking of Emotions, carried out by the participants throughout the week. The task consisted of daily recording of emotions using the practice of colors, both through writing and creative expression, coloring a square with the color corresponding to the primary emotion each day. To support understanding, therapists can reintroduce the previously used model of emotion tracking. The therapist should use a welcoming and affectionate demeanor with the group members and is attentive to which core emotional needs would need to be met at the moment.

The therapist also encourages participants to continue creatively adapting plans into their routines, emphasizing flexibility and intentional practice (even if imperfect) as essential elements for cultivating healthy habits. During this stage, the therapist can ask participants how it was to perform the activity and which emotions they identified, encouraging the sharing of experiences. In addition, they can explore the learning derived from the emotional record, analyzing identified emotional patterns and their impacts on mental health in everyday life. Finally, the therapist introduces the next activity, which will be focused on the association between schema modes and emotions.

Emotional Understanding of Schema Modes

Objectives: To understand, in a playful way and using characters from popular culture relevant to the participants, how modes can be associated with different emotional experiences.

Procedure: The intervention begins with each participant receiving a sheet of paper to connect different feelings and emotions to known characters from fiction, such as "Snape" from Harry Potter, who can represent shame and fatigue, or "Hulk," who can symbolize anger and irritation. This connection is made from the notes of the action plan, with each emotion felt in the last week (or at least the most striking) being associated with a character.

In the second stage, participants are guided to connect these representations to specific "modes," naming them. For example, the inner critic (oppressive sociocultural) mode can be associated with "Snape," while the overcompensatory mode can be represented by "Hulk." This process facilitates the association between emotional activation and modes, in a playful and didactic way. Therapists can take advantage of this dynamic to generate insights, explaining that some emotions and reactions reflect typical patterns of a specific mode, offering tips to help participants recognize when they are transitioning between different forms of functioning.

The activity seeks to stimulate creativity and bring understanding about schema modes, helping participants understand their functions. Group members are encouraged to create alternative and personalized names for the modes, if they feel that no character adequately represents them. For example, they can use names like "Little Dave" for a vulnerable child or "Wall" for an avoidant mode. Participants can also resort to the names defined in the action plan of the second meeting, refining and improving the "mode map" based on the knowledge acquired about themselves throughout the sessions.

The activity ends with a discussion in which participants reflect on the changes in their understanding since the first time they saw the mode map (in the second meeting) until the present moment. Do they notice more details about the functioning of their different parts? Can they emotionally connect with each of them? Do they have more clarity about their characteristics? This reflection helps to solidify the understanding of the modes and encourages continuous reflection on personal growth and development, as well as motivating them to recognize the new knowledge acquired about themselves.

Activity narration: “Bring to mind situations this week where you had strong emotions. Try to think about the details of each of them: where you were, who was with you, when they happened. Write on paper how you felt in these situations, even if these feelings are not something you are proud of. Now, consider that this ‘you’ in each situation represents a small part of who you are.

Bring to mind a character who shares the same feelings as this part of you. It can be Hulk or any other character from fiction. Write a small summary of who they are based on your feelings. For example, you can say: ‘Hulk is a grumpy and stressed guy, who is always arguing with everyone around him. He thinks everyone is annoying’.

Do this for all the emotions you can remember feeling this week. If you used emotion tracking, you can consult it now. Remember to include both pleasant and unpleasant emotions, avoiding focusing only on the negative.

Now, let’s remember the modes—these different internal parts that a person has—and connect them to the characters. Take the paper filled out in the second session, referring to the action plan. Which modes do you remember? (*The therapist waits for the participants’ response*). Very well, all of these are great examples. Shall we remember what they all are? If any mode does not fit a character or you prefer to use another name, feel free to create personalized names, like objects or nicknames. When you finish thinking and recording, we will discuss what has changed since the first time you saw this mode map. Our goal is to take advantage of everything we have learned throughout the sessions to refine this tool even more. What have our discussions and exercises brought to your understanding of your different internal parts?”

Chairwork Technique Using Balloons: Combating the Inner Critic (Oppressive Sociocultural) Mode

Objectives: To confront and disempower the inner critic (oppressive sociocultural) mode, promoting the protagonism of the participants.

Procedure: This activity, created based on Farrell and Shaw (2020) and Cardoso et al. (2022), aims to offer participants, now more familiar with the modes, the autonomy to represent them in a roleplay. To make the experience comfortable and avoid stigmatizing those who interpret modes seen as “negative” (such as the inner critic (oppressive sociocultural) mode), they will use balloons as symbolic representations of these parts. The participants, with the support of the therapist, will draw on the balloons the characteristics of the mode that will be represented by a volunteer. Thus, the personification of the mode is associated with the balloon and can be "removed" at the end of the activity. After the exercise, the balloons can be popped or discarded symbolically, as a symbol of emotional regulation and affirmation of the participants' progress.

Various combinations of modes can be worked on, including the representation of multiple modes in the same session, depending on the available time and readiness of the group. For example, a participant can narrate a challenging situation recently experienced, with chairs representing specific modes (such as the detached protector, the inner critic mode, and the vulnerable child), exploring their interactions in a fictional scenario. The following narration presents an example with the affirmative healthy adult mode dialoguing with the inner critic (oppressive sociocultural) mode, but the intervention can be adapted to other modes or contexts, according to the needs of the group.

Two important aspects should be observed: before starting the activity, the name of the inner critic (oppressive sociocultural) mode should be agreed upon with the volunteer participant to avoid confusion between the character represented and the personal identity of the participant. Although the focus of the intervention is the inner critic (oppressive sociocultural) mode and its relationship with issues related to the experience as a person of diverse sexual identity and/or sexual orientation, it is possible to explore self-criticisms from other areas brought by the participants, expanding the reach of the activity. The technique bears similarities to the exercise performed in Session 3, but offers greater autonomy and participation to the group.

Narration of the activity: Therapist: "Today, we will construct a dialogue between the inner critic (oppressive sociocultural) mode and the affirmative healthy adult. For this, we will place two chairs in front. We will use the example that [*volunteer's name*] brought. Let's start with you, representing the inner critic (oppressive sociocultural) mode, expressing something that this mode often tells you or makes you feel. Before we start, what would you like to call this critical side of yours? (*Pause to hear the answer*). Great! Let's use that name. Now, sit in the chair representing the '[*name of the inner critic (oppressive sociocultural) mode*]'."

Inner critic (oppressive sociocultural) mode (*volunteer with the balloon or mask on the face*): "You never do anything right. Why do you always fail? Others are better than you, and you will always be behind them. You are not good enough to be married or have children – you chose to date another woman/man. What will your parents think of you not being able to give them a family?"

Therapist (mediating): "These are very strong and quite cruel words, '[*name of the inner critic (oppressive sociocultural) mode*]'. This is not true or fair. Now, I ask that [*volunteer's name*] leave the '[name of the inner critic (oppressive sociocultural) mode]' in the chair, placing the balloon on it. Let's invite the affirmative healthy adult to respond. What is their name? (Pause for answer). Great, [*name of the healthy adult*]! Sit in the chair in front of the '[*name of the inner critic (oppressive sociocultural) mode*]'. What do you have to say in response? Remember to speak with understanding, strength, and self-care."

Affirmative healthy adult (volunteer): "I know that I have made mistakes throughout my life, but I have also learned from them. I am striving for better and growing. Comparing myself to others is neither fair nor useful. I am on my own path. My way of loving is not wrong. It is you, '[*name of the inner critic (oppressive sociocultural) mode) mode*]', who is trying to belittle me – you are the one who is wrong and problematic, not me. I can marry and have children, build a family, if I wish. Maybe not in the way my parents expected, but I can be happy and surrounded by people who love me."

Therapist: "Excellent! Let's continue this dialogue. '[*Name of the inner critic (oppressive sociocultural) mode*]', return to your chair. How do you respond to this?"

The therapist facilitates the dialogue, keeping it productive, and ensures that the healthy adult has the last word. If the inner critic (oppressive sociocultural) mode becomes dominant, the therapist can intervene directly, allying with the healthy adult as a good caregiver. The co-therapist should be attentive to possible emotional activations of the other participants and, if the group is well-integrated, others can join the dialogue with their healthy adults, using additional chairs.

After the exercise, the therapist promotes a group reflection, encouraging participants to share their learnings and discuss how to apply these insights in everyday life. The dialogue offers participants the opportunity to explore their own internal voices, with the therapist acting as a guide, providing support and encouragement, as well as asking guiding questions to keep the focus on the task. If time allows, other volunteers can narrate their own lived situations and experiment with the chairwork technique, expanding the benefits of the intervention for the group as a whole.

Feedback and Action Plan

The therapist should ask the participants how they felt during the activities carried out on the day and what they learned about themselves and their modes. The main objective of this meeting was to solidify the knowledge about each mode and the interactions between them, as well as to facilitate their recognition through emotions and physical sensations. Thus, questions directed at these aspects can be asked to assess whether the session achieved the expected results.

Next, the therapist introduces the action plan, explaining that the group will jointly create a soothing audio. They should clarify that the audio will serve as a reminder and a tool to help participants cope with modes that cause intense emotional activation, promoting an emotional change. The idea is to replace an unpleasant emotion, which arises during these activations, with a more pleasant and context-appropriate emotion, as exemplified in the chairwork exercise.

Each participant is encouraged to contribute a sentence or thought that helps them in difficult times. The therapist suggests that everyone reflect on what they intend to say before the recording begins. They should ensure that everyone understands the activity and feels comfortable participating.

The recording is made during the session, with the therapist facilitating the process and guiding the participants. They can start the audio with a mantra or a phrase that activates their healthy adult, inviting the others to continue the exercise. It is important to encourage participation and collaboration from everyone, remembering that each voice in the group has value and that each member's contribution is essential. The co-therapist can end the audio with their own speech. Participants are instructed to use the audio as a support tool in times of difficulty (or simply to comfort themselves and remember the group) during the following week, consolidating this resource as the action plan.

Action plan: listen, whenever necessary, to the soothing audio recorded in session by the group (use it as a resource to remember one's own value and promote comfort in times of need).

Appendices and materials needed for Session 9
– Balloons and pens for the relief balloon and chair technique activities.

References

Cardoso, B. L. A., Paim, K., Catelan, R. F., & Liebross, E. H. (2022). Minority stress and the inner critic/oppressive sociocultural schema mode among sexual and gender minorities. *Current Psychology, 42*, 19991–19999. https://doi.org/10.1007/s12144-022-03086-y

Farrell, J. M., & Shaw, I. A. (2012). *Group schema therapy for borderline personality disorder: A step-by-step treatment manual with patient workbook*. Wiley-Blackwell.

Further Reading

Cardoso, B. L. A., Lima, A. F. A., Costa, F. R. M., Loose, C., Liu, X., & Fabris, M. A. (2024). Sociocultural implications in the development of early maladaptive schemas in adolescents belonging to sexual and gender minorities. *International Journal of Environmental Research and Public Health, 21*(8). https://doi.org/10.3390/ijerph21080971

Farrell, J. M., & Shaw, I. A. (2012). *Group schema therapy for borderline personality disorder: A step-by-step treatment manual with patient workbook*. Wiley-Blackwell.

Farrell, J. M., & Shaw, I. A. (2018). *Experiencing schema therapy from the inside out: A self-practice/self-reflection workbook for therapists*. The Guilford Press.

Farrell, J. M., & Shaw, I. A. (2020). Creative use of mode dialogues with the vulnerable child and dysfunctional critic modes. In J. S. Heath & M. Startup (Eds.), *Creative methods in schema therapy: Advances and innovation in clinical practice*. Routledge.

Shaw, I. A. (2020). Spontaneity and play in schema therapy. In J. S. Heath & M. Startup (Eds.), *Creative methods in schema therapy: Advances and innovation in clinical practice*. Routledge.

van der Wijngaart, R. (2021). *Imagery rescripting: Theory and practice*. Pavilion Publishing & Media.

Young, J. E., Klosko, J. S., & Weishaar, M. E. (2003). *Schema therapy: A practitioner's guide*. Guilford Press.

Chapter 11
"Acting as the Person I Aspire to Be": Behavioral Strategies for Coping with the Inner Critic (Oppressive Sociocultural) Mode

The tenth session of the program aims at promoting behavioral changes related to patterns associated with the inner critic (oppressive sociocultural) mode. To achieve this goal, various strategies are used. Among them, assertiveness training stands out, which seeks to confront harmful self-criticism and assist participants in establishing their own boundaries in a healthy and effective way. The session also includes an in-depth analysis of individual behaviors and the stimuli that can trigger them, such as thought traps and schema activations. Through this analysis, participants gain a clearer understanding of the origins of their self-critical behaviors, identifying both healthy and dysfunctional coping strategies (Table 11.1).

Review of the Action Plan

The therapist asks participants how they felt hearing their own voices and those of their peers during the week, exploring what emotions or thoughts were evoked. This is an opportunity to promote an even deeper connection among group members. The therapist can also highlight the importance of continuity and consistency in using these tools, even after the group ends. They can reinforce that these resources will always be available, helping participants maintain a good quality of life and remember their shared learnings—what is taken away goes beyond the 12 meetings. The therapist encourages participants to use the audios in times of need or simply to comfort themselves and remember the group, whenever they wish or need. It is explained that, just like in the previous session, the connection with the modes will continue to be explored. Now that participants have developed a greater understanding of their various parts and are advancing in the regulation of thoughts and emotions, the focus of the current meeting will be to better understand their own behaviors and identify which ST resources can help them deal more effectively with these aspects.

B. L. A. Cardoso, A. C. G. Braga, *The PRISMAS Group Therapy Handbook*,
https://doi.org/10.1007/978-3-031-91809-4_11

Table 11.1 Session activities and estimated duration

Activity/intervention	Estimated duration
Review of the action plan	15 minutes
Therapeutic writing: recording emotionally important moments from the last week and how I reacted to them	25 minutes
Discussion on how our way of acting may be connected to our modes	30 minutes
Roleplay: assertiveness training	40 minutes
Feedback and action plan	10 minutes

Therapeutic Writing: Recording Emotionally Important Moments from the Last Week and How I Reacted to Them

Objectives: To regulate emotions and offer a healthy alternative to dealing with emotional activations.

Procedure: Therapists should distribute paper and pen to participants and guide the activity with the following instructions, asking them to imagine pouring their feelings onto the paper. There is no need to write well or coherently. There are no rules—the focus is to connect with emotions and express them through writing. Although the absence of rules may initially cause discomfort for some participants, the idea is precisely to allow freedom of expression. If someone feels lost, therapists can suggest the following examples:

1. Close your eyes, focus on the emotion, and write the first words that come to mind when you open your eyes, even if they seem incoherent.
2. Define five keywords related to the emotion and use them as topics to develop the text.
3. Write a poem that represents the feelings experienced at the moment.

At the end of the activity, if any participant offers to share their text, therapists should promptly thank, hold space for, and validate the contribution. The dialogue about the records can enrich the reflective process of all group members.

Narration of the activity: "Today we will carry out a therapeutic writing practice as our first exercise of the day to get us feeling more present. I want to invite all of you to settle into a comfortable position, grab paper and pen, and prepare to dive into an introspective journey. This activity is not about writing perfectly or as if you were an author, but about exploring and recording what you are feeling here and now. I will be here to guide you during the process and help in case of any confusion.

First, connect with what you are feeling. Pay attention to body sensations or the rhythm of thoughts. Consider what we learned in the last meeting and try to identify which mode is present now. Avoid judging emotions as good or bad at this moment; just feel them for a moment. (Pause). Now, pour these emotions onto paper, even if in a confused or incoherent way. Remember that you don't have to share what you wrote with anyone, not even with me, if you don't want to. This gives you the freedom to perform the exercise in a completely personal way. After finishing, we will tear up the sheets and throw them away.

You will have a few minutes in silence to write about everything that comes up, Again, don't worry about grammar or style; just let flow what comes to mind. Shall we start? Take a deep breath, relax, and allow yourself to enter this space of self-knowledge."

Discussion on How Our Way of Acting Can Be Connected to Our Modes

Objectives: To promote reflection on the dysfunctional coping modes used by participants and identify behavioral patterns associated with the inner critic (oppressive sociocultural) mode.

Procedure: The activity is centered on a group discussion. The therapist starts the conversation by encouraging participants to reflect on the different modes that cause intense emotional activations in their lives. Participants are encouraged to identify how they act when these modes are activated and to recognize the signs that indicate such activations. For example, a participant may report that, when they are in angry child mode, they typically feel intense anger, manifested by shouting and slamming doors. They are invited to share their experiences and reflections, illustrating how these modes affect their daily behaviors.

Then, the therapists propose to organize the shared information in an educational way. From the reported examples, the therapists can use a board or slide to structure the content in three columns. In the first column, they note recent situations in which participants felt intense emotional activation. In the second, they record the corresponding mode. Finally, in the third, they describe the behaviors presented in response to these emotions. After this initial organization, each participant is invited to record personal examples on a sheet of paper. Time is reserved for them to complete this process. This part of the session aims to encourage participants to develop a deeper awareness of their own reactions and behavior patterns. Special attention should be given to the inner critic (oppressive sociocultural) mode, which is the main focus of the intervention. An example of this activity can be seen in Table 11.2.

After completing this written reflection, the group explores three coping styles: resignation, overcompensation, and avoidance. They have been previously introduced in the thought traps activity and in the current meeting will be a greater focus. Resignation refers to accepting the negative situation without resistance, yielding to it without a fight. Overcompensation involves trying to overcome or control the situations, often through excessive or aggressive actions. Avoidance implies running away or denying the situation, trying to ignore it or hide it (including from oneself).

The therapist will explain each style again, associating the modes with them (e.g., the compliant surrender with resignation, the overcompensatory modes with overcompensation, and the avoidant modes with avoidance). It may be interesting to

Table 11.2 Example of application of the activity (situation, emotion, and behavior)

Situation	Perceived emotion	Behavior
"I met some colleagues on the street who have treated me badly and who I experienced bullying from at school because of my sexuality. I got upset"	Anxiety, restlessness (impulsive child mode)	As I was driving past them, I slowed down so I could shout at them that they were losers before speeding off (overcompensatory mode). Despite this, I arrived home feeling like that excluded child again
"I was dating a guy I liked a lot, and he told me that he is not out to his family, so he doesn't see himself in a serious relationship right now because of this, although he is willing to try more in the future"	Sadness, hurt, and shame (vulnerable child mode)	Faced with the feeling of inadequacy and helplessness, I cut off all contacts with the guy, to avoid suffering in case he didn't want to date me in the future, and I went to a club to hook up with other people and distract myself (avoidant modes)
"My boss asked me to work on the weekend, something that I don't notice him asking my colleagues. The entire team is composed of heterosexual men and I am the only lesbian woman. It's not the first time I feel undervalued in the company"	Anger, irritation (angry child mode)	I tried to suppress the anger, as I am in a risky position within a more conservative company. Even though my boss is open to conversations and asks me for feedback, I avoid speaking. There was one day, I ended up letting out some sarcastic comments, but I blame myself for the outburst and try not to show any discomfort, always doing overtime instead (compliant surrender mode)
"I see on social media that my friends went out on the weekend without me. I got bothered and started to think that they don't like me and find me weird and too flamboyant, being a more effeminate gay man"	Shame, loneliness (vulnerable child mode)	I keep repeating to myself that I am a failure and need to improve and that I am a mistake for being a LGBTQIA+ person. The intrusive thoughts become strong and constant, in a way that leaves me anxious and depressed (inner critic (oppressive sociocultural) mode)

use guided discovery and allow the participants themselves to make these associations, if possible—it is always more effective for participants to reach conclusions on their own in psychotherapeutic contexts.

It is worth highlighting to the participants that all coping modes arise in response to a need to protect the individual during their development. For example: a boy who always deals with invalidating parents, who criticize his way of acting (wearing nail polish), of speaking (with a socially considered more feminine tone), and of feeling (being emotional and sensitive) may start to enter the self-soothing protector mode, playing video games for hours on end in the early hours to avoid having to think or feel the suffering caused by those caregivers. A girl criticized by her peers for liking to play soccer and dressing in a way considered culturally more masculine may enter the overcompensatory mode, using clothes considered very feminine, even if she feels uncomfortable with them. The coping modes are briefly explained in Table 11.3, including some common characteristics to them.

Table 11.3 Coping modes, brief description, and some characteristics

Coping mode	Description	Some characteristics
Compliant surrender	Dysfunctional coping strategy in which the individual submits to others, repressing their own needs and desires to avoid conflicts	– Easy submission to others – Repression of personal needs – Unexpressed resentment and tension – Living with abusive behaviors without taking a stand – Persistent suffering in the long term
Avoidant	Strategies to avoid difficult and emotionally painful experiences, involving emotional disconnection or seeking immediate relief	Detached protector: – Emotional disconnection – Avoidance of intense emotions – Feelings of apathy, existential emptiness, boredom, somatization, and self-harm Self-soothing protector: – Seeking immediate relief – Behaviors such as compulsive shopping, compulsive sex, and excessive consumption of food, alcohol, and/or other drugs – Difficulty in effectively solving problems
Overcompensatory	Dysfunctional strategy of excessive effort to appear strong and capable, ignoring the limits of others and presenting authoritarian, grandiose, or perfectionist behaviors	Self-aggrandizer – Acts as superior to others. – Behaves in a selfish, controlling, and abusive manner – Believes that common rules do not apply to them Bully and Attack – Authoritarian and competitive posture – Uses threats and intimidation to achieve what they want – Seeks to control people through violence (psychological, moral, and others) Attention and approval seeker – Super focused on the validation and/or approval of others – Attempts to always be the center of attention – May relate to people only for the status that a particular individual has and/or will give them by being associated with them (including aesthetic and social standards) Overcontroller – Perfectionist and obsessive, focused on performance to avoid criticism – Hypervigilant, overly attentive to people, imagining that there is something wrong or suspicious about them Cunning/manipulative – Attempt at excessive control – Lies and deceptions to achieve objectives – May play the victim to avoid negative consequences and/or blame others

Source: Based on Rafaeli et al. (2011), Trapp (2024), Wainer and Rijo (2016), Young et al. (2003)

Participants are invited to reflect on how these modes manifest in their lives and to discuss in a group how they can identify and respond to their activations and triggers in a healthier way. Therapists can ask, for example, "what kind of behavior would I be proud to have in this situation?" or "is there any recent situation in which I remember dealing well with a similar thought or emotion?" The goal is to guide participants to describe possible, more functional strategies to react to their feelings, sensations, and thoughts, without invalidating or inhibiting them. Therapists can, also, give suggestions and models of healthy behavioral reactions to the different cases reported by the group, if they have difficulty in formulating ideas on their own. Creativity should be encouraged, with therapists suggesting that everyone list as many alternative options as possible, to evaluate together what would be the best course of action for each example provided later.

Finally, the inner critic (oppressive sociocultural) mode is once again explored, with participants trying to recognize their behavior patterns when they are in this specific mode. Therapists can try to summarize a general view of the group about the way they act in this mode. They can also inform that these perceptions will be important for the next activity, where participants will enact this mode. The clearer it is to them how it presents itself behaviorally, internally, and externally, the better.

The activity is concluded with a discussion on how to integrate this knowledge into daily life. The therapist encourages participants to consider how they could use this understanding to respond in a healthier way to situations that provoke intense activation. They can ask for suggestions of healthy coping mechanisms that the participants themselves already perform in their routines, also reinforcing their potential. It is important to note what is already good and can be amplified.

Roleplay: Assertiveness Training

Objectives: To explore and understand different communication styles, including assertive, aggressive, and passive; express anger in a healthier way, redirecting this feeling assertively to those who cross the participants' coexistence limits.

Procedure: The therapist begins the session by presenting the three communication styles:

- Assertive: expressing one's own feelings and thoughts in a clear, honest, and respectful way.
- Aggressive: tendency to violate the rights of others, with behaviors such as shouting, interrupting, and speaking in a sarcastic way.
- Passive: inability to express one's own thoughts and feelings, often leading to the invasion of personal boundaries.

After the explanation, therapists can encourage group members to reflect on which communication style predominates in their daily interactions. It is important to emphasize that there is no "perfect" style; in certain situations, being more direct may be necessary, while in other contexts (such as with an annoying boss), passivity may be the only viable way out. Assertiveness tends to be a flexible model, working well in several situations.

After this introduction, therapists can request that group members share situations where the inner critic (oppressive sociocultural) mode is activated by anger or leads them to feel this emotion. The discussion should aim to identify ways to channel this anger productively, using assertive communication, an effective behavioral strategy. Assertive communication involves the use of clear and respectful language, maintaining eye contact, and the controlled expression of feelings.

Narration of a roleplay model: "For the next intervention, we will stage a situation to demonstrate the difference between passive, aggressive, and assertive communication. I need a volunteer to help me. Does anyone volunteer?" (*The volunteer and the therapist sit in the center of the room*).

Therapist: "Now, imagine that you are my coworker and you are making unpleasant and biphobic comments to me, a bisexual person. You said things like 'you must be indecisive', 'you are straight, but want to appear trendy' or 'you're dating a person of the opposite gender, stop pretending to be bi!' We will roleplay my response to this scene three times. First, I will represent a passive person. Please, say some comments or microaggressions that you think a bisexual person could hear in their professional environment."

Volunteer: "Hey, you're indecisive, aren't you? And wanting to go along with these new trends of being "queer." Now it's cool to say you like everyone, but to date you went straight to choosing a man."

Therapist (*illustrating passively, speaking in a low and hesitant tone*): "Well, it's not quite like that… so, it might seem like indecision, but… you know how it is (*nervous laughter*)."

Psychoeducation from the therapist: "Given this response, perhaps you can to think that I took the offensive comment lightly, as if it was appropriate. Moreover, this can give the impression that I am an easy target for insults and unwanted jokes. I am allowing my space to be invaded without protecting myself."

Therapist talks about the next illustration: Now, I will respond aggressively to the same comment.

Volunteer: "Hey, you're indecisive, aren't you? And wanting to go along with these new trends of being "queer." Now it's cool to say that you like everyone, but for dating you went straight to choosing a man."

Therapist (*illustrating aggressively, speaking in an exalted manner, with a loud voice*): "Who do you think you are?! You're an idiot! How dare you say such a thing to me?"

Therapist's psychoeducation: "Although I am defending my rights and the complaint is valid, by responding in this way, I can end up creating a negative climate with colleagues. The person could use my overreaction as justification for a possible intervention from Human Resources, which would not solve the problem and, in the worst case, could make it seem like both sides were wrong, when in reality it was an undeniable, biphobic offense." Now, I will demonstrate how to respond assertively. Shall we try again?

Volunteer: "Hey, you're indecisive, aren't you? And wanting to go along with these new trends of being "queer." Now it's cool to say that you like everyone, but for dating you went straight to choosing a man."

Therapist (*illustrating the assertive way, speaking in a firm and clear manner, with a serious expression*): "I understand that you may see these comments as a joke, but for me they are not funny – I can't laugh at them. They hurt me, as they question an essential part of who I am. I would like to ask you not to make this type of comment anymore, okay? I like you and I don't want to have to resort to contacting Human Resources. If you want, we can also talk about jokes or topics that are sensitive to you, and I can commit to being more careful with them. Agreed?"

Therapist's psychoeducation: "As you can see, I kept my posture, voice and gaze firm, without giving room for my words to be disregarded. Often, it is necessary to maintain a serious climate to show that certain attitudes are inappropriate. However, as it is a work environment, it is important to be tactful when speaking, therefore, I brought up the importance of good coexistence before talking about seeking Human Resources. However, if the harassment continues, this would still be a valid option. To prevent the person from becoming defensive, I quickly suggest a commitment from both parties, showing an effort on my part to be attentive to the sensitive topics to my colleague. This helps to make the atmosphere more positive and creates an environment for dialogue."

After the presentation of the models of behavior styles, the participants are divided into pairs or small groups, where each one assumes a role in a scenario related to the inner critic (oppressive sociocultural) mode. One of the members represents the colleague, friend or unpleasant stranger, while the other responds assertively, switching roles afterward. They practice assertive communication, and the therapist and co-therapist circulate around the room, providing feedback, highlighting strengths and areas for improvement. The therapists can also offer individualized guidance to refine these skills.

Feedback and Action Plan

At the end of the meeting, feedback from participants about the session is sought once again. It is important to ask how they felt during the exercises and if they can imagine applying what they learned in new situations, generalizing these behaviors to other areas of their lives. They can also be asked about which factors could hinder this and how they could overcome these barriers and obstacles.

The action plan aims to promote a clearer awareness of how the inner critic (oppressive sociocultural) mode can influence the participants' behaviors. During the week, they are encouraged to pay attention to situations in which they acted and reacted guided by this mode. A common way of being directed by this mode is to perceive oneself as a mistake, inadequate, problematic, etc. (common anti-LGBT comments in society). Often, a moral or religious discourse internalized accompanies this mode, involving the internalization of negative speeches permeated by prejudice against sexual and gender diversity. Faced with these thoughts, a person can, for example, socially isolate themselves (thinking they will not be loved), direct anger at themselves (instead of actually responding to the offender), or even hurt themselves (repeating offenses to themselves in thought or self-harming). The goal is not only to identify these moments, but also to reflect on them and consider possibilities for healthier behaviors, being more attentive to who, in fact, should be the target of assertive anger. The participants will actively propose to use more functional strategies during the week.

Action plan: during the week, pay attention to situations in which you acted guided by the inner critic (oppressive sociocultural) mode and reflect on possibilities for different actions, actively using the more functional strategies developed in the session.

Appendices and materials needed for Session 10
– Blank sheets of paper for the therapeutic writing exercise – Printed sheets with the thought record model (Appendix VIII)

References

Rafaeli, E., Bernstein, D. P., & Young, J. (2011). *Schema therapy*. Routledge.

Trapp, R. (2024). "House" e "Lucifer": Deus e o diabo na terra da hipercompensação. In B. L. A. Cardoso & K. Paim (Eds.), *Terapia do esquema no cinema: os filmes e series na compreensão da prática clínica* (pp. 281–312). Artesã.

Wainer, R., & Rijo, D. (2016). O Modelo Teórico: Esquemas Iniciais Desadaptativos, Estilos de Enfrentamento e Modos Esquemáticos. In R. Wainer, K. Paim, R. Erdos, & R. Andriola (Eds.), *Terapia Cognitiva Focada em Esquemas: Integração em Psicoterapia*. Artmed.

Young, J. E., Klosko, J. S., & Weishaar, M. E. (2003). *Schema therapy: A practitioner's guide*. Guilford Press.

Further Reading

Cardoso, B. L. A., Lima, A. F. A., Costa, F. R. M., Loose, C., Liu, X., & Fabris, M. A. (2024). Sociocultural implications in the development of early maladaptive schemas in adolescents belonging to sexual and gender minorities. *International Journal of Environmental Research and Public Health, 21*(8). https://doi.org/10.3390/ijerph21080971

Cardoso, B. L. A., Paim, K., Catelan, R. F., & Liebross, E. H. (2022). Minority stress and the inner critic/oppressive sociocultural schema mode among sexual and gender minorities. *Current Psychology, 42*, 19991–19999. https://doi.org/10.1007/s12144-022-03086-y

Farrell, J. M., & Shaw, I. A. (2012). *Group schema therapy for borderline personality disorder: A step-by-step treatment manual with patient workbook*. Wiley-Blackwell.

Farrell, J. M., & Shaw, I. A. (2018). *Experiencing schema therapy from the inside out: A self-practice/self-reflection workbook for therapists*. The Guilford Press.

Farrell, J. M., & Shaw, I. A. (2020). Creative use of mode dialogues with the vulnerable child and dysfunctional critic modes. In J. S. Heath & M. Startup (Eds.), *Creative methods in schema therapy: Advances and innovation in clinical practice*. Routledge.

Shaw, I. A. (2020). Spontaneity and play in schema therapy. In J. S. Heath & M. Startup (Eds.), *Creative methods in schema therapy: Advances and innovation in clinical practice*. Routledge.

van der Wijngaart, R. (2021). *Imagery rescripting: Theory and practice*. Pavilion Publishing & Media.

Part III
Final Sessions: Consolidating and Strengthening My Affirmative Healthy Adult and Having Fun with My Happy Child

Chapter 12
"Connecting Our Individual Strengths to Health and Affirmation": Building the Healthy Adult Connected to the Social Group

In the eleventh session of PRISMAS, the focus is on building the healthy adult and their interconnection with social contexts, emphasizing the acceptance of sexual orientation and/or gender identity and the establishment of healthy relationships. The session unfolds into a series of interventions aimed at empowering participants, providing them with a safe space to explore their gender and/or sexual identity proudly, while fostering positive connections with the LGBTQIA+ community. The concept of "schema chemistry" is addressed, exploring how life experiences shape relational choices (for better or worse). The session seeks the creation of a collective model of healthy relationships, highlighting values such as mutual respect and open communication (Table 12.1).

Space of Affirmation Technique with Emphasis on Sexual Orientation and/or Gender Identity

Objectives: Strengthen the affirmative healthy adult; hold space for and affirming the group; performing space of affirmation technique again, now focusing on a space where the person is free to live their sexual orientation and/or gender identity and validated with pride by people from the LGBTQIA+ community.

Procedure: The therapist explains that the space of affirmation exercise will be repeated, this time with emphasis on pride and acceptance of one's own sexuality, as worked on throughout the meetings. It is about creating a safe space for participants to feel completely free to live their identity and sexual orientation. This place can be real or imaginary, but should preferably be significant for the person's identity as a sexual and/or gender minority. The therapists highlight that the current session seeks to affirm each participant's identity, with the support of peers and based on the bonds built during the group.

B. L. A. Cardoso, A. C. G. Braga, *The PRISMAS Group Therapy Handbook*,
https://doi.org/10.1007/978-3-031-91809-4_12

Table 12.1 Session activities and estimated duration

Activity/intervention	Estimated duration
Space of affirmation technique with emphasis on sexual orientation and/or gender identity	25 minutes
Review of the action plan	15 minutes
Understanding how our life story can influence our relational choices	35 minutes
Collective construction of a model of relationships based on the healthy adult	35 minutes
Feedback and action plan	10 minutes

Narration of the activity: "Close your eyes or keep your gaze downward, whichever is most comfortable for you at this moment. Direct your attention to your breathing, allowing it to slow down. (Pause). If you notice tension in any part of your body, simply allow it to relax. If thoughts arise during the exercise, don't worry. Just let them go gently and return to the image I am about to describe. (Pause).

Now, slowly allow the image of a Place of Pride and Acceptance to emerge in your mind. This is a safe space where you can fully live your sexual orientation (or gender identity) and be exactly who you are, without fear, shame, or punishment. Here, you are valued in your entirety, exactly as you are. It can be a real or imaginary place, but it is even more meaningful if this place symbolizes your identity and the LGBTQIA+ population. Let the image of this place form naturally. (Pause). Now, observe the details of this environment. What are the colors that compose it? What textures can you feel? What objects are present? And what is the lighting like? (Pause). Perhaps this place has various LGBTQIA+ symbols. Or, perhaps, it is a simple place, but where you feel comfortable, safe and free. (Pause).

Now, listen to the sounds around. What kind of music or sounds can you perceive? Focus on a sound that feels affirmative for you—perhaps a song that inspires and empowers you. (Pause). And what is the smell you associate with this place? Focus on an aroma that you associate with positivity and well-being. (Pause).

Allow yourself to stay in this Place of Pride and Acceptance for a few minutes, absorbing as much as you can. Feel the joy and lightness of being connected to your essence and authenticity. (Pause). If you wish, you can invite someone to be with you in this scenario. It might be interesting to have other LGBTQIA+ people around. It could be someone from the group you trust—or even all of us! (Pause). You can also mentally invite people who are positive examples from the community for you. These companions should reinforce even more the feeling of belonging and well-being. (Pause).

Stay here, experiencing this scene, knowing that you can return to it whenever you need trust, support, and validation. (Pause). Now, slowly, allow the image to fade as you return your attention to breathing. (Pause). Take a deep breath and, when you're ready, gently begin to move, slightly turning your neck or stretching. Open your eyes in your own time, returning to our current space."

Review of the Action Plan

Therapists initiate the discussion of the action plan proposed in the previous week. They ask participants how the process of executing the task went and what each person's experience was in observing the inner critic (oppressive sociocultural) mode in everyday situations. They may question, for example, whether they are noticing greater ease in identifying this mode, understanding their own behaviors when they are under its influence and if they have greater clarity to choose how to act, knowing it has been activated. It is interesting to explore whether the participants were able to try out healthier behaviors and how they can generalize these learnings to other areas of their lives. In addition, the therapists can question about possible obstacles faced when trying to apply what was learned, as well as strategies to overcome these barriers in the future.

This activity provides an opportunity for participants to express their difficulties, successes, and attempts, while the therapists offer feedback and guidance to expanding the toolbox of coping skills. Taking advantage of the reflection on the action plan, therapists introduce the idea that the behaviors chosen in the face of each mode or schema can directly influence the relationships that people establish. Thus, being more connected to healthy modes and healthier ways of acting contributes to the construction of an affirmative support network—a central aspect of the current session.

Understanding How Our Life Story Can Influence Our Relational Choices

Objectives: To present the concept of "schema chemistry"; understand how life experiences shape the schemas and, consequently, the choices and relational interactions; understand the origin of interpersonal problems; manage some of these difficulties.

Procedure: The concept of "schema chemistry" refers to the way how early maladaptive schemas interact and shape our choices and relational interactions. Each person has a unique life story that influences the formation of their schemas, determining their beliefs, perceptions, and emotions. These schemas, in turn, guide the relational choices, leading people to seek situations and relationships that confirm and reinforce what is familiar to them, even if these things are dysfunctional or harmful (Cardoso & Paim, 2024; Rafaeli et al., 2011; Stevens & Roediger, 2016; Young & Klosko, 1994). For example, someone may be attracted to a partner uninterested in them because it reminds them of a negligent caregiver in childhood. Schema chemistry consists of choices that activate emotional pains and that do not meet emotional needs adequately (Cardoso & Paim, 2024). To explain this, therapists can reintroduce the concept of schemas as smaller parts that make up a mode.

To illustrate, consider a person with an "abandonment" schema, resulting from caregivers who were rarely present or died prematurely. They may be prone to choosing unstable or emotionally unavailable partners, perpetuating the cycle of loneliness without realizing it. A partner with an "emotional inhibition" schema, created in a rigid and conservative environment, may be attracted to people with these same characteristics. Both would be in a relationship causing suffering, but attractive due to its familiarity. This dysfunctional dynamic is reinforced by the illusion that, in trying to avoid abandonment, one of the partners (overcompensation) can scare the other, who in response tries distancing themselves even more (avoidance), perpetuating emotional pains. The pains persist in the attempt to do differently, if they are not looked at and cared for with affection.

A metaphor that may be interesting to illustrate this concept is the "toothpaste versus cleaning pill": "Imagine that, after years using toothbrushes and toothpaste, a fantastic scientific discovery emerges: brushing your teeth is bad! The solution would be to take a cleaning pill that solves all dental problems. Despite being more advantageous, many people would resist the change, while children, who grew up with the new solution, would quickly adhere. This reflects the discomfort we feel when abandoning familiar patterns, even if they are healthier." This example illustrates how dysfunctional relational patterns can be challenged and changed.

A suggestion to make the activity dynamic is to ask for the participants to share stories of "bad dates" or "toxic friendships"—adapting the names to those popularly used at the time when this program is being applied. These commonplace terms are usually used to describe situations where schema chemistry led to unhealthy choices. This facilitates therapist and participants understanding each other. They can take advantage and ask to tell a little about how they believe their life story and the story of the other party involved (if they know it) may have impacted this relational attraction. If it is difficult for members to think about this at first, therapists can give examples, as a way to model behavior.

Understanding schema chemistry can provide reflections for patients about how their life stories influenced their relational choices and how the schemas may have interfered in their relations. Through the recognition of these patterns, participants begin to challenge and change maladaptive schemas, allowing them to make healthier and more satisfying relational choices in the future.

Collective Construction of a Model of Relations Based on the Healthy Adult

Objectives: To provide participants with a practical view of how to seek healthy relationships in their lives; to empower participants to build healthier and more satisfying relationships in their support network.

Procedure: This intervention follows an approach similar to the "good caregiver" intervention. It begins with a request for participants to identify the characteristics and behaviors that represent their healthy adult selves. Although they have already done this in more detail previously, they should now write down on a piece of paper the strengths they have cultivated over the weeks of intervention, as well as the behaviors they are still developing and wish to continue cultivating after the group ends. The idea is that this should be done briefly, to avoid repetition—it is not the focus of the session, but a way to reinforce the other points to be worked on in the activity.

Next, each participant should write their healthy and unhealthy relational patterns on the same sheet, to have a broader view of what works and what does not work in their interpersonal relationships. The goal is for them to be honest when writing, without the need to share aloud what they have recorded, if they do not wish to.

The therapists aim for the group to recognize both what they have received and offered in their relationships, without judgments. The intention is not to feed self-criticism, but rather to allow an honest and transparent look at what has not been working and what works in their own relationships. It should be noted that there is no completely perfect friendship or love and everyone will always have points to improve as friends and partners.

The therapists continue the discussion, asking questions like "We talked in the previous exercise about schema chemistry and what negative qualities can actually deceive us in attraction. Now, how about we talk about the qualities that attract us and that are positive? Can anyone give an example?" or still "Let's think together about what a relationship between healthy adults would be like, that is, a responsible, mature, safe and affectionate relationship. And its opposite: a relationship that does not meet emotional needs. What do you suggest would be qualities, emotions, habits, etc. present in each of them?"

Based on the responses brought by the participants, the therapists can explain that good relationships meet core emotional needs: the offering of secure attachment, the setting of healthy boundaries, the promotion of autonomy, the cultivation of play, and the validation of emotional expressions. On the other hand, unhealthy relationships do the opposite: they generate insecure attachment (constant anxiety or avoidance), lack boundaries (dysfunctional emotional dependence), curtail autonomy (excessive jealousy, abusive restrictions), lack spontaneity and play (criticism of the way of being and the tastes of the other person), and promote emotional invalidation (not listening or embracing what the other brings, diminishing the importance of the partner's feelings).

Therefore, a healthy romantic relationship is one in which both parties demonstrate mutual respect, open and honest communication, and commitment to personal and relationship growth. It is important that the parties are sincere, vulnerable, open to criticism and to personal development, and that they have fun and quality time together. The responsibility to take care of one's own demands, both work and emotional, without overburdening the other, is fundamental. Finally, consistency and constancy help to create a secure base for this relationship. An adult in a healthy relationship is capable of:

- Offering secure attachment: Is emotionally available for the partner or friend, offering comfort, security, and support. This creates an environment where love, trust, and intimacy can bloom.
- Setting healthy boundaries: Expresses their needs and desires clearly and assertively, respecting others' boundaries, contributing to a balanced and respectful relationship. Assertive communication, previously trained in the group, is a great element for respectful and effective dialogue.
- Promoting autonomy: Encourages the partner to pursue their own interests and to develop their individuality. Both should strive to improve as individuals while still sharing a life together. Presence is essential for the other to feel that they have a safe harbor to return to, but excess can take away a certain level of freedom, which is essential for the relationship to breathe.
- Cultivating play: Values the time spent together, whether in fun or relaxing activities. It is important that the relationship has room for joy and humor, even if there are duties and obligations of adult life.
- Validating emotional expressions: Recognizes and validates the emotions of the other person, showing empathy and understanding. Being able to see the other as a unique individual who has their own wants and desires. Does not live only for them, just as they do not expect the other to dedicate only to the relationship. Both are capable of orienting themselves toward themselves when necessary, while still keeping the relationship as a priority.

It is not absolutely necessary to read to the patients what is written in this manual— the idea is that these concepts serve as a basis for understanding, with each therapist organizing and exploring what the group itself brings as healthy and functional relationships. It is emphasized once again that there is no perfect relationship and that everyone will have some difficulties at certain points, as well as greater ease at others. The activity allows everyone to have in mind a guide of what a healthy relationship is, using this knowledge as a "map" to help in the construction of a better experience with their own support network in the future. The therapists can, if it makes sense for the group, mention that the relationships built over the past few months are examples of experiences capable of adequately nourishing each one's emotional needs. This shows that everyone present is capable of living functional relationships.

Feedback and Action Plan

Therapists ask participants to share their thoughts and feelings about the session. As the focus of this session was mainly relational, it might be interesting to request not only some feedback, but to hear the opinions of all participants, reminding them they are in a safe place and this group is a support network for everyone. If it is comfortable for the members currently present, the therapists can ask each one to share their experience of participating in group therapy with their peers, highlighting the gains in sharing this space with similar people.

It is important to emphasize that this will be the last feedback on a specific session, as the next meeting is intended for the closure of the therapeutic process, when the intervention as a whole will be discussed. After collecting the feedback, the therapists propose the action plan for the next meeting.

Therapists ask each participant to bring, next week, a text, an image, or a poem that symbolizes the experience they had in the group and what therapy meant to them. It can be something created by the participant themselves—which is strongly encouraged—or something created by someone else, as long as it aligns with their vision of the past weeks. Therapists should encourage freedom and creativity in carrying out this activity, reminding that there are no right or wrong answers—it's an opportunity to unleash the inner child again.

The goal is for each one to express their experiences, feelings, and perceptions in a way that makes sense to them. Even those who have not fulfilled any previous action plan are encouraged to complete the final exercise. Therapists can reinforce that the exercise is not only intended for their own learning and change, but also as a way to express their gratitude for their peers and for the exchanges made in the group. As seen in the meeting, bonds are essential for mental health, and the idea is to celebrate the process experienced by everyone and the achievement of having followed through to the end.

Action plan: Bring a text, image, or poem (which can be made, encouraged, or taken from someone else) that symbolizes the experience in the group.

Appendices and materials needed for Session 11
– Sheets of paper for the collective construction exercise of models of relationships based on the healthy adult
– Printed sheets with a summary of each of the 18 early maladaptive schemas (Appendix XIX)

References

Cardoso, B. L. A., & Paim, K. (2024). *Armadilhas da química amorosa: aprenda com a terapia do esquema a identificá-las e encontre relacionamentos saudáveis*. Artmed.

Rafaeli, E., Bernstein, D. P., & Young, J. (2011). *Schema therapy*. Routledge.

Stevens, B. A., & Roediger, E. (2016). *Breaking negative relationship patterns: A schema therapy self-help and support book*. Wiley-Blackwell.

Young, J. E., & Klosko, J. S. (1994). *Reinventing your life: The breakthrough program to end negative behavior and feel great again*. Plume.

Further Reading

Cardoso, B. L. A., Lima, A. F. A., Costa, F. R. M., Loose, C., Liu, X., & Fabris, M. A. (2024). Sociocultural implications in the development of early maladaptive schemas in adolescents belonging to sexual and gender minorities. *International Journal of Environmental Research and Public Health, 21*(8). https://doi.org/10.3390/ijerph21080971

Cardoso, B. L. A., Paim, K., Catelan, R. F., & Liebross, E. H. (2022). Minority stress and the inner critic/oppressive sociocultural schema mode among sexual and gender minorities. *Current Psychology, 42*, 19991–19999. https://doi.org/10.1007/s12144-022-03086-y

Farrell, J. M., & Shaw, I. A. (2012). *Group schema therapy for borderline personality disorder: A step-by-step treatment manual with patient workbook*. Wiley-Blackwell.

Farrell, J. M., & Shaw, I. A. (2018). *Experiencing schema therapy from the inside out: A self-practice/self-reflection workbook for therapists*. The Guilford Press.

Farrell, J. M., & Shaw, I. A. (2020). Creative use of mode dialogues with the vulnerable child and dysfunctional critic modes. In J. S. Heath & M. Startup (Eds.), *Creative methods in schema therapy: Advances and innovation in clinical practice*. Routledge.

Shaw, I. A. (2020). Spontaneity and play in schema therapy. In J. S. Heath & M. Startup (Eds.), *Creative methods in schema therapy: Advances and innovation in clinical practice*. Routledge.

van der Wijngaart, R. (2021). *Imagery rescripting: Theory and practice*. Pavilion Publishing & Media.

Young, J. E., Klosko, J. S., & Weishaar, M. E. (2003). *Schema therapy: A practitioner's guide*. Guilford Press.

Chapter 13
"Releasing the Happy Child": Allowing the Expression of Creativity and Fun for the Group's Closure

In the twelfth and final session, participants are led through a series of therapeutic activities with the aim of promoting the closure of the group in a playful and fun way, activating the happy child. The therapists use imagery that allows participants to symbolically set aside stress and heavy emotions, focusing on the group experience. As a way to honor the time spent together, the tasks performed in the previous session are read and presented, emphasizing the authentic expression of the experiences lived. Then, the participants are guided in a memory drawing exercise, encouraging the creative expression of emotions related to group experiences. This practice is performed again in the last activity, a visualization that brings out the playful side of each participant, creating a light and cheerful environment to mark the end of the group meetings. The session highlights the importance of self-expression, reflection, creativity, and celebration of the relationships built, in addition to the experiences shared in the therapeutic group (Table 13.1).

Backpack Exercise

Objectives: based on Farrell and Shaw (2012), this exercise aims to provide emotional relief and relaxation to participants.

Procedure: The activity begins with the therapists guiding the participants through an imaginative sequence. The backpack practice is a symbolic way of demonstrating that, even though the participants are carrying stresses and heavy emotions, they have the ability to set them aside during the session, allowing them to fully focus on the group experience and therapeutic interventions. This practice is a preparation for the subsequent activation of the happy child. The therapists can praise the fact that the group has reached this last meeting, emphasizing that it will be a light and fun session.

B. L. A. Cardoso, A. C. G. Braga, *The PRISMAS Group Therapy Handbook*,
https://doi.org/10.1007/978-3-031-91809-4_13

Table 13.1 Session activities and estimated duration

Activity/intervention	Estimated duration
Backpack exercise	20 minutes
Reading and presentation of last week's action plan	45 minutes
Memory drawing exercise	30 minutes
Final exercise: amusement park	25 minutes

Activity narration: "To start this exercise, I invite everyone to find a comfortable position in their chairs and close their eyes. Breathe deeply a few times and let the focus shift from the external environment to your own inhale and exhale. (Pause). Count a couple breathing cycles, allowing your mind to quiet down.

Now, I want you to imagine yourself entering this room. There is no one in it yet - you were the first to arrive (Pause). You are carrying a backpack on your back. It's a backpack of your favorite color, very beautiful, well made. You feel its weight on your back. It is loaded with everything you brought with you here today - maybe fatigue, stress, anger, sadness, intrusive thoughts, work deadlines, worries or anything else you are feeling or thinking. (Pause).

You can see yourself sitting in your chair, gently placing your backpack on your lap. Take a moment to feel its weight, recognizing what you have been carrying with you. (Pause). There is no judgment here, just recognition.

Finally, imagine yourself placing the backpack on the floor, under your chair. Feel your shoulders become lighter, your neck and back relax, your legs also free and calm. (Pause). Recognize this feeling of relief, of having gotten rid of an important weight. You have not eliminated these things; they are still there, in your backpack, but now you are giving yourself a break, a moment to just be here and now, with lightness and peace. (Pause).

Gradually, each of us enters the room. First, I enter with my (*therapist's favorite color here*) backpack. I sit next to you, smile at you and also leave my backpack under the chair. (Pause). Now, (*name of co-therapist*) enters. They sit near us, with their (*co-therapist's favorite color*) backpack and places it under the chair as well. (Pause). Gradually, each of your colleagues enters the room and does the same action. Try to visualize each of them. (Pause).

After we are all together, let the image slowly fade away. (Pause). When you are ready, breathe deeply a few times and finally, open your eyes and turn your attention back to the group. (Pause). Remember that the backpack remains under your chair, allowing you to be present and fully participate in the today's activities."

Reading and Presentation of the Action Plan from the Previous Meeting

The therapists lead the review of the action plan proposed the previous week. In the task, each participant was asked to prepare a text, an image, or a poem that could symbolize the experiences lived in the group. In addition, each member was encouraged to feel free to create their own material, expressing their experiences and feelings authentically. The therapists can start by talking about their experience in conducting those meetings, emphasizing the positive points, the lessons they took away, and the challenges they overcame. Each of them should also present their text or image, made manually, to serve as a model for the participants. They can also affirm that, despite the inherent shame of speaking in public, they are in a safe space and that finishing this process together is a reason for pride.

The tone of voice adopted by the therapists should be gentle, recognizing the vulnerability that may be associated with this type of self-expression. The therapists emphasize again that the goal is for each one to express their feelings and individual perceptions in a way that makes sense to themselves, reinforcing that there are no right or wrong answers.

At this moment, the therapists invite the participants to share, one by one, what they brought and to explain the reason for choosing that specific material. As the participants share their experiences, the therapists offer incentives and thanks, validating individual experiences. The goal is to create a safe space for everyone to feel comfortable expressing themselves and reflecting on the shared experiences. The therapists recognize and validate the courage needed for this activity. Finally, they conclude this part of the session, thanking each one for their willingness and participation. From this task, they introduce the idea of, together, carrying out a final expressive and fun activity to activate the happy child.

Memory Drawing Exercise

Objectives: Promote reflection, emotional expression, and interpersonal connection among participants; consolidate and celebrate the group's shared journey.

Procedure: The activity begins after the action plan review, as an active complement. The therapists guide the participants to sit on the floor, in a circle, to create a more informal and relaxed environment. This symbolic gesture aims to awaken each one's "happy child." They can explain that, after all the emotions felt in the sharing among peers, it is time to express even more creativity and the impact that group psychotherapy had on their lives.

Next, a variety of colored pens or pencils, as well as papers, are distributed among the participants. The participants are guided to connect with the feelings, sensations, and thoughts evoked by the farewell texts and to reflect on how the group affected and marked them. At this point, the therapists highlight the freedom and the possibility of playful exploration that the use of various colors provides, allowing the participants to feel more at ease to express their emotions and experiences in a creative and uncomplicated way. The therapists themselves join the activity and create their own drawings, showing that they are an integral part of the group.

The participants are encouraged to use this reflection and the associated emotions as inspiration for their drawings. The therapists reinforce that the idea is not to create an aesthetically perfect work of art, but to produce a symbolic, affective, and meaningful representation of the experience with the group. The final drawing will be a memory that they will take home and can keep, allowing them to connect to the process whenever they want. If it is comfortable for the group, they can even exchange the papers among themselves, each taking the drawing of a colleague or therapists.

The therapists guide the participants to work in silence, allowing each one to dive into their own reflection and creative process. During this time, they offer encouragement and support as needed, respecting each one's individual space. At the end of the agreed time, the therapists invite the participants, one by one, to share their drawings and to explain what they represent, if they feel comfortable. At this moment, it is emphasized that each representation, like each experience, is unique and valuable and that each shared reflection contributes to the enrichment of the group as a whole.

Final Exercise: Amusement Park

Objectives: Stimulate the "happy child" mode even more in each participant; create a light and cheerful environment to end the session and the therapeutic group meetings.

Procedure: This exercise includes an imagery that invites the participants to imagine themselves in an amusement park, with all the tickets paid for by the therapists. The therapist should explain that they will generate a mental image intended to activate their playful side, ending the time they spent together in a fun and cheerful way. The participants should be encouraged to enjoy the exercise without shame or inhibition, focusing instead on the pleasure and simple joy that is typical of childhood.

Activity narration: "Let's start this exercise by closing our eyes and breathing deeply. Gradually, bring to mind the story I'm going to tell. We are very happy with what we built throughout our group. And we got tickets for all of you in an amusement park - it's a free pass. (Pause). You have the right to try all the attractions, as everything's totally free! And it's not just any regular park - it's the most exciting in the city. Together, we all go to this magical place, and when we arrive at the park, which is colorful and vibrant, the day is beautiful, sunny and pleasant. (Pause). We enter and receive our bracelets that gives us access to all the attractions.

The employee tells us that we can choose any ride we want, without restrictions. There are countless attractions, all exciting and fun. (Pause). For me, I decided to go first on the Ferris wheel (the therapist describes the experience on the Ferris wheel or another ride they like). What is the first attraction you choose? How was it to go for a ride on it? (Pause). We walk together through the park, laughing and talking, trying out each attraction we choose. (Pause). I'll give you a few minutes to imagine yourself going on each ride of your preference! It can be a very calm and pleasant one or perhaps one that's more exhilarating. (Pause).

At the end of the day, we are satisfied and tired - but full of joy and gratitude. (Pause). We take with us the feeling of happiness. Slowly, picture the end of our time at the park. (Pause). Gradually, let the image fade and return to paying attention to your breathing. (Pause). When you feel ready, open your eyes."

After the end of the narration, the therapists begin the closing discussion. They express gratitude to the participants and recap the work done so far. They thank for the trust placed in that experience and the gains perceived in the group, being genuine in their points. To demonstrate the shared humanity to the therapeutic process, they talk about what they learned and received with that experience. Each participant's journey, the significant moments that emerged, and the deep exploration of schemas and modes are recognized and celebrated.

Concluding the intervention, the therapists reinforce the purpose of the group and the importance of the work done, encouraging the continuity of learning, even without the weekly meetings. The therapists highlight the importance of the shared experience, wishing that the perceptions and learnings acquired flourish in all areas of the participants' lives. They open space for those who feel comfortable to share how that last activity was and use the remaining time of the session for free conversations and exchanges.

Appendices and materials needed for Session 12
– Sheets of paper for the drawing exercise, as well as colored pencils, markers, or crayons.

References

Farrell, J. M., & Shaw, I. A. (2012). *Group schema therapy for borderline personality disorder: A step-by-step treatment manual with patient workbook*. Wiley-Blackwell.

Further Reading

Cardoso, B. L. A., Lima, A. F. A., Costa, F. R. M., Loose, C., Liu, X., & Fabris, M. A. (2024). Sociocultural implications in the development of early maladaptive schemas in adolescents belonging to sexual and gender minorities. *International Journal of Environmental Research and Public Health, 21*(8). https://doi.org/10.3390/ijerph21080971

Cardoso, B. L. A., Paim, K., Catelan, R. F., & Liebross, E. H. (2022). Minority stress and the inner critic/oppressive sociocultural schema mode among sexual and gender minorities. *Current Psychology, 42*, 19991–19999. https://doi.org/10.1007/s12144-022-03086-y

Farrell, J. M., & Shaw, I. A. (2018). *Experiencing schema therapy from the inside out: A self-practice/self-reflection workbook for therapists*. The Guilford Press.

Farrell, J. M., & Shaw, I. A. (2020). Creative use of mode dialogues with the vulnerable child and dysfunctional critic modes. In J. S. Heath & M. Startup (Eds.), *Creative methods in schema therapy: Advances and innovation in clinical practice*. Routledge.

Rafaeli, E., Bernstein, D. P., & Young, J. (2011). *Schema therapy*. Routledge.

Shaw, I. A. (2020). Spontaneity and play in schema therapy. In J. S. Heath & M. Startup (Eds.), *Creative methods in schema therapy: Advances and innovation in clinical practice*. Routledge.

van der Wijngaart, R. (2021). *Imagery rescripting: Theory and practice*. Pavilion Publishing & Media.

Young, J. E., Klosko, J. S., & Weishaar, M. E. (2003). *Schema therapy: A practitioner's guide*. Guilford Press.

Chapter 14
Final Considerations

This manual was designed to assist therapists in directing intervention sessions with sensitivity and effectiveness. Throughout the manual, the aim was to present detailed descriptions of each session, outlining therapeutic objectives and procedures of practical activities, with the goal of enriching the development of therapists' clinical skills and improving the quality of life of LGBTQIA+ patients. To create an accessible logical line, concepts were gradually introduced, using applied interventions to solidify learning. It is recommended that therapists perform self-therapy and role-play with colleagues before applying the PRISMAS program, practicing the techniques and understanding them not only cognitively, but also experientially, before reproducing them externally.

Group Schema Therapy aimed at SGM individuals represents a therapeutic approach directed at assisting LGBTQIA+ people, adapting to their reality and context. In their journeys, these people face specific challenges and obstacles, and are often neglected by science and the public health system. When addressed, they usually have a negative perspective, due to minority stress. Therefore, this manual maintains an optimistic and positive stance, without neglecting the critical sense about living in a society that reproduces prejudice against sexual and gender diversity. Furthermore, it seeks to create a safe and welcoming space through the therapy interventions for SGM individuals to express themselves without fear. Thus, they can empower themselves with knowledge in a light way, understanding the anxieties that permeate their lives, through the understanding of maladaptive schemas and modes and the oppressive culture that formed them. The intervention's primary scope is to foster resilience, raise self-esteem, and cultivate acceptance of oneself and others. With this, the alleviation of symptoms such as anxiety, stress, and depression is expected.

In the initial stages, the emphasis is on creating a safe and welcoming environment where participants can share experiences and emotions without fear of judgment or discrimination. The integration between ST and Affirmative Therapy provides excellent tools for creating a genuine and strengthened therapeutic bond,

B. L. A. Cardoso, A. C. G. Braga, *The PRISMAS Group Therapy Handbook*,
https://doi.org/10.1007/978-3-031-91809-4_14

through limited reparenting. From this base, a gradual and gentle process of exploring the modes that influence the participants' existence can begin, aiming to identify patterns of thought, emotions, and behaviors that may harm their mental and emotional health. The Inner Critic (Oppressive Sociocultural) Mode and the Affirmative Healthy Adult Mode are especially highlighted for being directly associated with the experience of SGM.

During the intermediate sessions, various therapeutic techniques, such as imagery rescripting, chairwork, dramatization, therapeutic writing, and group discussions, are employed to facilitate a deeper understanding of the modes, in addition to developing new skills and strategies to deal with them. The importance of social connection and mutual support among participants is emphasized, facilitating the process and promoting autonomy in the group.

At the end of the intervention, it is essential that therapists reinforce the purpose of the group and the significance of the work done, encouraging the continuity of the therapeutic process and the application of the skills and strategies acquired throughout the group, in daily life. The focus is for participants to be able to enjoy the knowledge and skills learned, becoming, in this way, their own healthy adult role models and meeting their own emotional needs. It is important that therapists encourage participants to internalize the lessons learned and apply them in everyday life, strengthening their independence and resilience.

For the evolution of the ST for SGM, it is crucial that this intervention be constantly tested. This includes more research on the program, including its evaluation in different modalities (face-to-face and/or online), formats (group and/or individual), and audiences (e.g., with trans, non-binary, asexual people), in addition to the possibility of applying this model in a longer-duration group version (with more sessions). The possibility of further research and adaptations of this intervention is also highlighted, including its conceptual basis (understanding the inner critic oppressive sociocultural and affirmative healthy adult modes), for other marginalized social groups that still require greater attention in ST.

It is hoped that this manual will be a valuable tool for therapists, contributing to improving the quality of life of their LGBTQIA+ patients. It also serves as a gateway to diversity and inclusion. It is recommended that therapists who have their first contact with this subject (or with ST in general) seek other sources to expand their knowledge. Getting here, in reading this manual, demonstrates commendable effort and dedication.

Group ST for SGM not only seeks the individual improvement of LGBTQIA+ patients, but also the construction of a community of support and mutual understanding. During the sessions, participants have the opportunity to share their experiences, challenges, and achievements, creating a sense of friendship and belonging. This social connection is vital, especially for those who may not have consolidated support networks, essential for mental health and well-being.

Additionally, Group ST for this audience, although it has consistent elements to maintain its suitability, is a flexible approach that can be adapted to the specific needs of each group and individual. Therapists should be open to adjusting activities and techniques according to participant feedback and changes in life circumstances.

Finally, the dissemination of this therapeutic approach among the community of therapists and mental health professionals is essential to expand its positive impact. Continuous training, exchange of experiences, and sharing of best practices are vital to ensure that ST for SGM continues to evolve and meet the constantly changing needs of the LGBTQIA+ community. The ongoing commitment to cultural sensitivity and updating knowledge and consistency are keys to long-term success.

Further Reading

Cardoso, B. L. A., Lima, A. F. A., Costa, F. R. M., Loose, C., Liu, X., & Fabris, M. A. (2024). Sociocultural implications in the development of early maladaptive schemas in adolescents belonging to sexual and gender minorities. *International Journal of Environmental Research and Public Health, 21*(8). https://doi.org/10.3390/ijerph21080971

Cardoso, B. L. A., Paim, K., Catelan, R. F., & Liebross, E. H. (2022). Minority stress and the inner critic/oppressive sociocultural schema mode among sexual and gender minorities. *Current Psychology, 42*, 19991–19999. https://doi.org/10.1007/s12144-022-03086-y

Farrell, J. M., & Shaw, I. A. (2012). *Group schema therapy for borderline personality disorder: A step-by-step treatment manual with patient workbook*. Wiley-Blackwell.

Farrell, J. M., & Shaw, I. A. (2018). *Experiencing schema therapy from the inside out: A self-practice/self-reflection workbook for therapists*. The Guilford Press.

Farrell, J. M., & Shaw, I. A. (2020). Creative use of mode dialogues with the vulnerable child and dysfunctional critic modes. In J. S. Heath & M. Startup (Eds.), *Creative methods in schema therapy: Advances and innovation in clinical practice*. Routledge.

Meyer, I. H. (1995). Minority stress and mental health in gay men. *Journal of Health and Social Behavior, 36*(1), 38–56. https://doi.org/10.2307/2137286

Meyer, I. H. (2003). Prejudice, social stress, and mental health in lesbian, gay, and bisexual populations: Conceptual issues and research evidence. *Psychological Bulletin 129*(5), 674–697. https://doi.org/10.1037/0033-2909.129.5.674

Pachankis, J. E., Harkness, A. R., Jackson, S. D., & Safren, S. A. (2022). *Transdiagnostic LGBTQ-Affirmative Cognitive-Behavioral Therapy: Therapist Guide*. Oxford University Press.

Pachankis, J. E., & Safren, S. A. (Eds.). (2019). *Handbook of evidence-based mental health practice with sexual and gender minorities*. Oxford University Press.

Rafaeli, E., Bernstein, D. P., & Young, J. (2011). *Schema therapy*. Routledge.

Shaw, I. A. (2020). Spontaneity and play in schema therapy. In J. S. Heath & M. Startup (Eds.), *Creative methods in schema therapy: Advances and innovation in clinical practice*. Routledge.

van der Wijngaart, R. (2021). *Imagery rescripting: Theory and practice*. Pavilion Publishing & Media.

Young, J. E., Klosko, J. S., & Weishaar, M. E. (2003). *Schema therapy: A practitioner's guide*. Guilford Press.

Appendix I: Brief Description of Schema Modes

Child Modes

- *Vulnerable child mode:* This mode is characterized by painful memories and emotions from childhood, such as fear and insecurity. When activated, the person seeks protection and security, often feeling excluded or rejected in relationships. When in this mode, the person expresses their needs in a direct and emotional way, with physical and behavioral manifestations that include distress, accelerated breathing and facial expressions of sadness and insecurity. Its needs include support, validation and secure attachment.
- *Undisciplined/impulsive child mode*: This mode is characterized by resistance to rules and limits, often rooted in experiences of restriction or lack of limits in childhood. When in this mode, the person can engage in hasty and impulsive behaviors, in search of immediate gratification, potentially putting the person or others at risk. Despite appearing irreverent or defiant, it needs healthy limits to achieve emotional regulation.
- *Angry child mode:* This mode is characterized by intense emotions of anger and frustration, often originating from experiences of injustice or emotional abuse in childhood. When in this mode, the person may experience emotional outbursts and aggressive behaviors. They need emotional validation for anger and a safe space to vent their emotions. Physically, this mode can show itself through redness in the cheeks and a feeling of heat.
- *Happy child mode*: This mode is characterized by light and joyful feelings, associated with memories of positive moments from childhood. When in this mode, the person may experience feelings of joy, curiosity and spontaneity, promoting pleasure in simple activities and valuing contentment. People in this mode usually present themselves as smiling and laughing, with an innocent joy. Recognizing this mode is essential to balance the demands of adult life with moments of leisure and happiness.

B. L. A. Cardoso, A. C. G. Braga, *The PRISMAS Group Therapy Handbook*,
https://doi.org/10.1007/978-3-031-91809-4

Inner Critic Modes

- *Inner Critic Mode:* This mode is characterized by internalizations of criticism, punishments, and high demands from people who were part of the individual's life history (e.g., father, mother, grandparents, teachers, among others). The person in this mode experiences self-demands and self-punishments for general aspects of their own experience (e.g., work, studies, performance), but not necessarily in relation to their gender identity and/or sexuality.
- *Inner Critic (Oppressive Sociocultural) Mode:* This mode is characterized by oppressive and anti-LGBT internalizations. The person experiencing this mode holds negative beliefs about oneself, and this contributes to low self-esteem. They experience excessive self-demand and a distorted view of identity. When in this mode, the person focuses on a low self-worth related to their sexuality.

Dysfunctional Coping Modes

- *Compliant Surrender Mode:* This mode is characterized by easy submission to others, avoiding expressing needs. It focuses on the needs of others to avoid conflicts, generating resentment.
- *Avoidant Modes:* These modes are characterized by emotional disconnection from challenging situations (detached protector) and search for immediate relief (self-soothing protector). It avoids painful experiences and can result in dysfunctional behaviors such as addictions.
- *Overcompensatory Modes:* Self-aggrandizer: This mode is characterized by attempts to exalt oneself to deal with insecurities, demonstrating arrogance. Bully and Attack: Uses intimidations and threats for control, ignoring the needs of others. Attention/Approval Seeking: Focuses on external validation, reflecting feelings of inferiority. Perfectionist Overcontroller: Presents extreme perfectionism, seeking to avoid criticism, but results in emotional exhaustion. Conning and Manipulative: Uses lies and manipulations for control, affecting trust in relationships.

Affirmative Healthy Adult Mode

- This mode is characterized by the maintenance of a realistic and balanced perspective, making assertive decisions. Takes responsibility for their actions and takes care of their needs. Integrates vulnerability with reason, promoting emotional self-regulation. For LGBTQIA+ people, it embodies the internalization of positive messages about identity, countering social stigma. This mode can symbolize empowerment and emotional balance.

Appendix II: Mind Map of the Inner Critic (Oppressive Sociocultural) Mode

What Is the Inner Critic (Oppressive Sociocultural) Mode?

The inner critic (oppressive sociocultural) mode is the internal voice that judges us and makes us feel inadequate. It arises from negative messages received throughout life, such as criticism, prejudice, and social pressures related to our gender identity and/or sexual orientation. This mode reflects oppressive patterns present in society, influencing the way we see ourselves and how we relate to the world. It says as much about what we think about ourselves and the way we deal with the prejudice we receive, as about the external experiences of oppression we experience, such as microaggressions in the educational or health system, for example. It is an internalization of these pains, specific to people belonging to minority groups.

Origins of the mode:

- Messages of oppression received from society since childhood and adolescence;
- Negative comments about appearance, behavior, or abilities, for being an LGBTQIA+ person;
- Sociocultural pressures about sexuality, race, and social status;
- Gender stereotypes and distorted messages about gender roles;
- Imposition of unrealistic standards of beauty, success, and/or behavior (with increased effort demand for marginalized social groups);
- Experiences of stigma and discrimination;
- Experiences of prejudice or exclusion.
- Negative messages internalized as a result of rejection episodes or hearing negative comments about a personal characteristic or about the identity as an LGBTQIA+ person.

B. L. A. Cardoso, A. C. G. Braga, *The PRISMAS Group Therapy Handbook*, https://doi.org/10.1007/978-3-031-91809-4

Main characteristics when in this mode:

- Thoughts of self-criticism and self-hatred may arise, such as: "I am a bad and wrong person for being LGBTQIA+"; "The way I express my sexuality is inadequate"; "People will reject me if I am myself"; "My sexuality is a problem"; "I will suffer severe divine punishment, for being LGBTQIA+".
- Associated emotions: Shame, guilt, fear, anxiety, sadness, self-directed anger.

Impacts on physical and mental health:

- Increase in symptoms of stress, anxiety, and depression;
- Reinforcement of negative views about oneself and feelings of inadequacy and failure;
- Unhealthy reactions, such as avoiding these cognitions through substance abuse;
- Decrease in self-esteem and negatively distorted self-perception;
- Difficulties in interpersonal relationships and in establishing deep bonds, along with constant fear of rejection or abandonment;
- Sexual problems derived from high levels of anxiety and self-blame.

Some strategies to overcome the inner critic (oppressive sociocultural) mode:

- Identify and name the thoughts of the mode—thus, we can realize when it is present and not believe and trust completely in all the information it communicates to us.
- Learn to counter self-criticism—an effective strategy is to raise signs contrary to that thought, as if we were collecting evidence for a jury and bringing a more honest and complete view of the situation. Thus, we get out of the tendency to focus only on the negative.
- Ask yourself: "Is this voice mine or was it something I learned?"—one of the characteristics of the inner critic (oppressive sociocultural) mode is the excess of identification with what is thought, as if it were an absolute truth. Reflecting on the origin of that criticism helps in cognitive defusion; that is, better understanding that thoughts are just phrases that repeat and do not necessarily reflect what we really are or believe.
- Focus on your achievements, skills, and unique qualities—remembering moments of success, when it is common to think about failures, helps to balance and counterbalance this internal dialogue.
- Maintain relationships that promote support and encouragement—the companies that surround us can significantly impact the way we see ourselves. Being in front of reinforcing and welcoming people is a way to maintain a good view of ourselves. If the people we have as support and reference belong to the population of sexual and gender minorities, this becomes even more powerful, as it helps us to question imposed standards and to seek diverse and inclusive presences.
- Affirm yourself! There is nothing wrong with you being who you are. Your gender identity and sexual orientation are valid expressions of your experience.

Appendix III: Coping Card

Coping cards are a practical extension of Thought Record (TR). They summarize the learnings and strategies to facilitate quick use in challenging moments, reinforcing healthy thoughts and constructive behaviors. The following will present tips on how to create your coping card according to the proposal of Young et al. (2003).

How to create your coping card?

- *Step 1:* Identify the negative thought—Use the TR structure to recognize thoughts that arise in times of difficulty. Guiding questions in the face of an activating situation: "What scenes come to my mind at this moment? Does any specific memory appear? Do I attribute any characteristics to myself? Does the way I see the world and the people around me change?". For example: "I am a mistake for being a LGBTQIA+ person".
- *Step 2:* Identify the underlying schema—Connect the thought to a maladaptive schema that may be activated. You can find a summary of them in Appendix X. For example: Schema of Defectiveness/Shame.
- *Step 3* : Restructure the thought—Replace the negative thought with a more balanced and healthier alternative. Here, it's not about thinking positive all the time, but rather trying to have a more honest and gentle look at reality. For example: "There is nothing wrong with me being an LGBTQIA+ person, my emotions and my identity are valid. The mistake lies in prejudice and in society that reproduces it and not in who I am."
- *Step 4:* Include examples of real evidence—Consider situations that prove the healthy view, strengthening it. For example: "I know other people who are like me. Science confirms that there is nothing wrong with me being an LGBTQIA+ person and that this is natural. These kinds of thoughts only arise when I remember what I've heard from a part of society that is prejudiced and this part cannot define my whole life".

B. L. A. Cardoso, A. C. G. Braga, *The PRISMAS Group Therapy Handbook*, https://doi.org/10.1007/978-3-031-91809-4

- *Step 5:* Define a behavioral instruction—Base yourself on the healthy thought to create a positive alternative action. For example: "Despite this thought coming up sometimes, I know it is wrong and has not helped me to have good mental health. I will seek help from professionals and friends whenever necessary and I will affirm myself daily, until this becomes the real feeling."

Appendix IV: Characteristics of the Healthy Adult

Who is the Healthy Adult?

The Healthy Adult is the functional, mature, and balanced part of each one of us. They regulate emotions and behaviors adaptively, helps to establish healthy relationships and promotes problem-solving in a practical and constructive way. As part of the therapeutic group, we have two main goals: to disempower and combat the Inner Critic (Oppressive Sociocultural) Mode and to strengthen the Affirmative Healthy Adult, that is, the part within us linked to pride, self-esteem, and self-love. So that we can learn to bring it more and more to the fore (yes, the Healthy Adult already exists within you! Maybe it just needs to come out little by little, with care), it is important to know its main characteristics and relevant qualities.

You are in Healthy Adult mode when:

1. You are aware of your beliefs, needs, values, and feelings.
2. You feel that you are the one who regulates your feelings and needs—not that you are controlled, impulsively, by them.
3. You can maintain your values, beliefs, feelings, and needs even in the presence of people who emotionally activate you (such as a figure of authority or someone who makes you insecure).
4. You can clearly express your feelings, beliefs, and emotional needs without apologizing, minimizing, or hesitating.
5. You maintain a constant internal sense of "Self" in all situations and circumstances, without confusion about what you really feel or want. You have clarity and pride in who you are.
6. You pursue meaningful personal values, living according to your worldview.
7. You have an internal sense of "centering", especially during times of stress. You can organize your own head when the situation calls for it (as in family or work crises, for example).

B. L. A. Cardoso, A. C. G. Braga, *The PRISMAS Group Therapy Handbook*, https://doi.org/10.1007/978-3-031-91809-4

8. You have clear boundaries between yourself and others, being able to connect and, at the same time, maintain autonomy.
9. You can maintain your own self-esteem and a positive and coherent view of yourself, without needing to depend on what others say about you.
10. You can adopt an assertive stance on issues that matter, taking a stand.
11. You can trust your intuition and feelings, without doubting yourself and your own perceptions.
12. You are proud of who you are and can feel comfort and validation about your sexuality (and this includes your gender identity and sexual orientation).

It is important to note that, although you may not have these 12 points well developed immediately, they are dimensional and are always under construction. In this way, you become healthier each day as you focus on learning the skills you lack and learn to use the best of the potential you have already built within you.

How to strengthen the Healthy Adult?

1. Practice self-reflection: identify areas of your life where you can apply the characteristics of the Healthy Adult and try, as much as possible, to repeat the behaviors that bring you closer to your real identity. It's like going to the gym: the more we perform the same movement, the more it becomes effective and our muscles get stronger and more powerful.
2. Invest in self-care: take care of your physical, emotional, and mental health regularly. We can only be healthy if we have time, space and energy for it. Don't blame yourself if you're overwhelmed—part of being healthy is recognizing the limitations of the context and taking care of yourself in these moments.
3. Challenge negative thoughts: question negative beliefs or internal criticisms that make you doubt yourself.
4. Cultivate positive relationships: build and maintain connections that encourage emotional support and mutual respect.
5. Seek continuous learning: participate in activities or therapies that strengthen emotional and problem-solving skills.
6. Set priorities and realistic goals: focus on objectives that reflect your values and bring personal fulfillment, in a didactic, clear and intentional way.
7. Connect with other people from the LGBTQIA+ community; this can strengthen your social support and allow you to share common experiences, facilitating your affirmation.

Appendix V: Brief Summary of the Five Core Emotional Needs (CENs)

The core emotional needs (CENs) represent essential pillars of healthy human development and directly influence our ability to build a balanced and meaningful life. These needs include aspects such as emotional connection, freedom of expression and autonomy, which form the basis for our mental health and interpersonal relationships. When met, they promote stability, creativity and well-being, helping people to cope with challenges and to achieve personal fulfillment.

However, when the CENs are not adequately met, early maladaptive schemas can arise—mental and emotional patterns that lead to negative thoughts, painful emotions and can impact the choice of harmful behavioral strategies. These schemas often develop in childhood, from experiences of invalidation or emotional neglect, and persist throughout life, harming mental health and relationships with others. Schema Therapy aims to identify and modify these patterns, helping us to meet our needs in a constructive way, even in adult life and in the present. There are five CENs, according to the model of Schema Therapy (Young et al., 2003).

1. **Secure Attachment/Connection**
   a. What it is: Refers to the need for emotional connection with others people, including protection, care, stability, empathy and understanding. A relationship with loving and consistent caregivers during childhood is essential to create a sense of security and trust.
   b. Schema domain when not met: Disconnection and rejection—when the need for secure attachment is not met, feelings of isolation, loneliness and fear of rejection and/or abandonment arise. People may believe they are unworthy of love or support.

2. **Autonomy, Competence and Sense of Identity**
   a. What it is: Represents the ability to feel confident to make decisions, explore the world and function independently. Children encouraged to make choices

B. L. A. Cardoso, A. C. G. Braga, *The PRISMAS Group Therapy Handbook*,
https://doi.org/10.1007/978-3-031-91809-4

with support develop skills to solve problems and adapt to the demands of adult life.

b. Schema domain when not met: Impaired autonomy and performance. The lack of support to develop autonomy can lead to feelings of incompetence, excessive dependence or exaggerated fear of failure.

3. **Realistic Limits and Self-Control**
   a. What it is: Refers to the ability to establish internal boundaries, respect rules and take responsibilities in a balanced way. Growing up with clear, healthy boundaries, contextualized to a particular moment in life, and appropriate consequences, helps in the development of discipline and self-control.
   b. Schema domain when not met: Impaired limits—individuals who do not develop realistic boundaries may have difficulties in respecting norms, regulating behaviors or recognizing the needs of others.

4. **Emotional Validation and Freedom to Express**
   a. What it is: It involves the need to have your emotions, thoughts, and needs recognized, validated, and respected. When a child has the freedom to express their emotions, they learn to communicate and establish healthy relationships.
   b. Schema domain when not met: Other-Directedness—emotional invalidation can lead people to ignore their own needs to please others, resulting in a weak sense of identity.

5. **Spontaneity and Play**
   a. What it is: Refers to the ability to be creative, explore the world and enjoy leisure without excessive demands or restrictions. Moments of play and relaxation during childhood contribute to the development of emotional balance and creativity.
   b. Schema domain when not met: Overvigilance and inhibition—individuals who do not develop spontaneity may become excessively critical, inhibited, or unable to relax and enjoy life.

Appendix VI: Thought Traps

- **Personalization:** A form of distorted thinking that involves attributing external events to oneself, as if the blame for something broad was your responsibility. For example: "I am to blame for my family's suffering because I am gay/lesbian/bisexual/trans." Imagining that any sadness or discomfort of loved ones is your fault and your gender identity and/or sexual orientation, ignoring the sociocultural factors of prejudice against sexual and gender diversity.
- **Catastrophizing (fortune telling):** A form of distorted thinking that involves expecting the worst possible scenario will occur, often exaggerating the consequences of a situation. For example: "I will be extremely rejected by my friends and family and will be unable to fully live my sexuality as an LGBTQIA+ person." This thought predicts a catastrophic negative outcome in relation to the person's personal future, due to their sexual orientation and/or gender identity. This interpretation may ignore the friends who would really support them and/or the new friendships that could be built more aligned with who they really are.
- **'All or nothing' thinking:** A form of distorted think that involves seeing situations in an extremist way (black or white), without recognizing their nuances. For example: "If I don't get the highest grade, I'm a complete failure. Because I am a person of the LGBTQIA+ community, I need to compensate in some way." This attitude ignores the possibility that there are many levels of success and failure, and that a grade below perfection does not mean total failure. Also, it is a trap by diminishing one's own achievements in view of their gender identity and/or sexual orientation.
- **Disqualifying or discounting the positive:** A form of distorted thinking that involves rejecting or minimizing positive experiences, attributing them to luck, coincidence or external circumstances, instead of recognizing one's own merit or positive qualities. For example: "I got the job, but it was only because of the diversity campaign, not because I was especially qualified." This perspective disregards the effort, skills, or qualifications that may have contributed to success, attributing it entirely to external factors.

B. L. A. Cardoso, A. C. G. Braga, *The PRISMAS Group Therapy Handbook*,
https://doi.org/10.1007/978-3-031-91809-4

- **Emotional reasoning:** A form of distorted thinking that involves letting emotions dictate conclusions, without objective analysis. For example: "People even say that I'm interesting, but I feel inadequate and uninteresting" The person, in this case, may be stuck to their own perception and not identify that this is just a thought that does not correspond with reality.
- **Labeling:** A form of distorted thinking that involves generalizing mistakes or specific behaviors as absolute definitions about oneself or others. For example: "I'm bisexual, so I need to have a very active love life." This thought has an inadequate idea of what bisexuality is. It is common for people to confuse concepts such as gender roles (acting in a more socially feminine or masculine way), sexual behavior (having few or many partners) and sexual orientation, although one thing does not necessarily relate to the other.
- **Magnification/Minimization:** A form of distorted thinking that involves amplifying negative aspects and diminishing the positives in a situation, especially when they relate to one's own achievements. For example: "I only got the promotion because no one else wanted the job. I made several mistakes in the process". It is common for sexual and gender minorities to discredit their own achievements and have lower self-esteem than average, even though they are competent. Therefore, they may minimize their qualities and success, focusing on the negative points.
- **Mental filter (selective abstraction):** A form of distorted thinking that involves focusing only on the negative of a situation, ignoring the positive. For example: "Since I couldn't have a good date [even though I've had other good dates], this means that I am a terrible person." This statement ignores several positive aspects that have already occurred and filters the information in a way that leaves only a view that one is a terrible person due to the last date.
- **Tunnel vision:** A form of distorted thinking that involves seeing only the negative aspects, ignoring alternatives, usually with a pessimistic bias. For example: "My friend didn't greet me properly; he must be disappointed with me or angry." In this type of thinking, the person may ignore the other possible alternatives for this situation, such as the friend being busy or going through personal problems, for example.
- **Mind reading:** A form of distorted thinking that involves assuming that you know what others they are thinking. For example: "He didn't respond to my 'good morning'; he must find me annoying." The best way to know what other people are thinking is to ask them what they are thinking. By assuming that we know what they are thinking, we can make mistakes in thoughts that are not compatible with reality.
- **Overgeneralization:** A form of distorted thinking that involves turning an isolated experience into a broad rule. For example: "Since I was rejected by this person I'm getting to know, no one else will find me interesting and/or want anything to do with me." In this way of thinking, there is an unfair generalization that all relationships and/or encounters will be bad and that no one will be interested in the person.

- **'Should' and 'must' statements:** A form of distorted thinking that involves imposing rigid expectations on oneself or others. For example: "I should handle everything alone; asking for help is weakness." This way of thinking ignores that social contact and asking for help are part of the human experience. Asking for help does not make a person a failure, but is a common human experience for everyone.

Appendix VII: Color Emotion Diary

Date	Most felt emotion	Color*	Reflections about it
09/13/2024	Sadness	Black	"I felt very sad this day, as I was procrastinating a lot and realized that I delayed my tasks"
09/14/2024	Joy	Green	"It was a calm and enjoyable day, as I managed to handle my tasks. I realized that having an organized day greatly helps my mood"

B. L. A. Cardoso, A. C. G. Braga, *The PRISMAS Group Therapy Handbook*,
https://doi.org/10.1007/978-3-031-91809-4

Appendix VIII: Thought Record

Recognizing the problem and formulating strategies (self-monitoring): The Thought Record (TR) is an important technique to identify negative automatic thoughts, understand their origins and replace them with healthier alternative thoughts. This technique helps to reduce the influence of maladaptive schemas and to promote healthy behaviors.

Situation (What happened?)	
Automatic Thought (What immediately went through your head?)	
Emotion (What did you feel?)	
Evidence supporting the thought	
Evidence against the thought	
Alternative or balanced thoughts	

B. L. A. Cardoso, A. C. G. Braga, *The PRISMAS Group Therapy Handbook*,
https://doi.org/10.1007/978-3-031-91809-4

Appendix XIX: Brief Summary of the 18 Early Maladaptive Schemas

(Based on Cardoso et al., 2024)

Emotional Deprivation: Belief that one will not receive the necessary emotional support from the people around. For example: "Nobody will ever love or accept me if I reveal my true gender identity or sexual orientation."

Abandonment/Instability: Belief that one will not have stable and secure connections. For example: "My friends will abandon me if I come out as LGBTQIA+.", "My relationships will never work out, no matter how hard I try".

Mistrust/Abuse: Expectation that others will hurt, abuse, or take advantage of oneself. For example: "People know about my sexual orientation just by looking at me and that's why they are always trying to deceive me.", "People will betray me because of who I am".

Defectiveness/Shame: Belief of being inadequate or that something is wrong about who one is. For example: "The fact that I am attracted to people of the same gender (or have a different gender identity) shows that I am a dirty and shameful person.".

Social Isolation/Alienation: Feeling that one is different from others or that one does not fit into spaces and contexts. For example: "As a bisexual person, I am 'too straight' for the gay community and 'too gay' in heterosexual spaces."

Failure: Belief that one will fail and feel inadequate in achievements. For example: "No matter how hard I try, being an LGBTQIA+ person I will always fail."

Dependence/Incompetence: Belief that one is incapable of handling daily responsibilities alone. For example: "I can't do anything, I always need help.", "I am incompetent to achieve my goals in a heteronormative society".

Vulnerability to Harm or Illness: Belief that an imminent catastrophe (physical, financial etc.) will happen. For example: "As an LGBTQIA+ person, it's very easy to go bankrupt, get sick or have some health problem, so I need to always be prepared for the worst."

B. L. A. Cardoso, A. C. G. Braga, *The PRISMAS Group Therapy Handbook*,
https://doi.org/10.1007/978-3-031-91809-4

Enmeshment/Underdeveloped Self: Excessive emotional involvement with significant people due to difficulty in self-validation. For example: "I need my parents and they wouldn't cope without me. I can't leave home to live my sexuality."

Entitlement/Grandiosity: Belief of being superior to other people or deserving special treatment. For example: "I am better than other LGBTQIA+ people and deserve to be treated in a special way".

Insufficient Self-Control/Self-Discipline: Difficulty in seeking long-term reinforcements, and low tolerance for frustration. For example: "I can't stop being late for work - I stay up until dawn watching series every day."; "Self-discipline is only for heterosexual people".

Self-Sacrifice: Sacrificing oneself for the sake of others, even if it brings suffering. For example: "I put the needs of others before mine and that's being a good person."

Subjugation: Excessive submission to others for fear of suffering retaliation or being abandoned. For example: "It's better to hide my sexuality, so that I won't be excluded or criticized."

Approval-Seeking/Recognition-Seeking: Need for others' approval to feel valued. For example: "I need the approval and recognition of people about my sexual orientation and/or gender identity."; "I need people to recognize how good I am".

Emotional Inhibition: Belief that feelings should be expressed in a veiled way, difficulty in connecting with emotions. For example: "I don't understand why my boyfriend keeps asking me to show that I like him, when I've already said it once."; "It's not right to show that I like a person of the same sex as me".

Unrelenting Standards: Pursuit of high standards and difficulty in being flexible. For example: "I have to be perfect in everything to be accepted, since I am an LGBTQIA+ person."

Negativity/Pessimism: Extreme focus on negative aspects and denial of positive aspects. For example: "Nothing in my life goes right, everything will always go wrong because I am LGBTQIA+."

Punitiveness: Belief that one should be punished or that others deserve punishment for perceived mistakes. For example: "It's better never to tell anyone about my sexual orientation, nor do anything about it or I might go to hell."

Index

A

Affirmative therapy, 1, 8, 9, 125
Assertiveness training, 9, 99, 100, 104–106

C

Chairwork, 9, 38–43, 91, 92, 94–96, 126
Cognitive techniques, 125
Core emotional needs, 3, 4, 28, 58, 61, 75, 87, 93, 115

E

Early maladaptive schemas, 1–6, 113, 117
Emotional regulation, 4, 9, 18, 32, 61, 78, 83, 91, 95

G

Group Schema Therapy, 125

H

Happy child, 10, 27, 29, 75–78, 119–123
Healthy adult, 8, 10, 16, 25, 27, 31–32, 37–42, 49–59, 61, 66, 76, 87, 95–97, 111–117, 126

L

LGBTQIA+, 6, 10, 31, 45, 51, 52, 69, 72, 102, 111, 112, 125–127
Limited reparenting, 17, 75, 126

M

Minority stress, 8, 29, 37–46, 125

S

Schema modes, 6–8, 17, 25, 27, 32, 34, 37, 92–94
Schema therapy, 1, 8, 9
Self-monitoring, 8, 9, 15–17, 68, 77
Sexual and gender diversity, 1, 6, 7, 41, 69, 107, 125
Sexual and gender minorities, 1, 29, 37–46, 49, 69

B. L. A. Cardoso, A. C. G. Braga, *The PRISMAS Group Therapy Handbook*,
https://doi.org/10.1007/978-3-031-91809-4

MIX
Papier aus verantwortungsvollen Quellen
Paper from responsible sources
FSC® C105338

If you have any concerns about our products,
you can contact us on
ProductSafety@springernature.com

In case Publisher is established outside the EU,
the EU authorized representative is:
Springer Nature Customer Service Center GmbH
Europaplatz 3, 69115 Heidelberg, Germany

Printed by Libri Plureos GmbH
in Hamburg, Germany